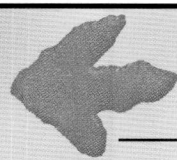
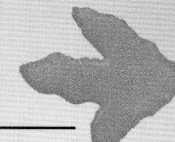

# DINO STORIES

# TYRANNOSAURUS

## TYRANT LIZARD

### ILLUSTRATED BY JAMES FIELD

## A&C BLACK • LONDON

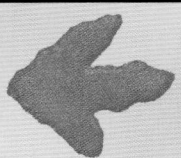

DINO STORIES TYRANNOSAURUS, TYRANT LIZARD
was produced by

**David West 🕱 Children's Books**
7 Princeton Court
55 Felsham Road
London SW15 1AZ

*Designed and written by* Rob Shone
*Editor:* Gail Bushnell
*Consultant:* Steve Parker, Senior Scientific Fellow, Zoological Society of London

*Photographic credits:* Postdlf, 5t; Quadell, 5bl; iStockphotos.com/Christoph Ermel, 30.

*First published in the UK in 2007*
*by* A&C Black Publishers Ltd
37 Soho Square
London W1D 3QZ
www.acblack.com

Copyright © 2007 David West Children's Books

This book is produced using paper that is made from wood grown in managed, sustainable forests. It is natural, renewable and recyclable. The logging and manufacturing processes conform to the environmental regulations of the country of origin.

11 10 09 08 07
10 9 8 7 6 5 4 3 2 1

ISBN: 978 0 713 68609 8 (hardback)
ISBN: 978 0 713 68619 7 (paperback)

A CIP catalogue record for this book is available from the British Library

*Words in bold appear in the glossary*
*Printed and bound in* China

# CONTENTS

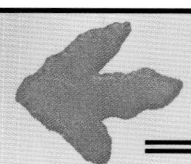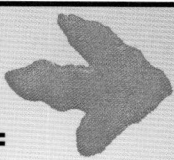

# WHAT IS A TYRANNOSAURUS?

## *TYRANNOSAURUS* MEANS TYRANT LIZARD

◄ *Tyrannosaurus had a good sense of balance and hearing.*

◄ *Tyrannosaurus had a keen sense of smell.*

◄ *It had large eyes that faced forwards. This helped it to judge distance.*

◄ *A long, stiff tail acted like one side of a see-saw to balance Tyrannosaurus' massive head.*

◄ *Tyrannosaurus' 1.5 metre (5 ft) jaws held between 50 and 60 teeth. Each one grew up to 0.15 metres (0.5 ft) long. Their teeth often fell out but were replaced with new ones throughout their lives.*

◄ *Tyrannosaurus' legs had to be strong to carry its huge weight.*

◄ *Like all the Tyrannosaurs, Tyrannosaurus had tiny arms.*

TYRANNOSAURUS REX LIVED AROUND 70 TO 65 MILLION YEARS AGO, DURING THE **CRETACEOUS** PERIOD. **FOSSILS** OF ITS SKELETON HAVE BEEN FOUND IN NORTH AMERICA.

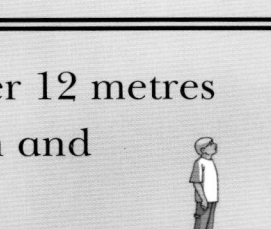

◄ An adult Tyrannosaurus was over 12 metres (40 ft) long, 5 metres (16 ft) high and weighed 6,800 kg (6.8 tons).

## GROWING UP

Tyrannosaurus rex grew at a steady rate until it was about 13 years old. For the next four or five years it gained 2 kilos (4.4 lbs) in weight a day. In that time it went from weighing 1,000 kilos (1 ton) to over 5,000 kilos (5 tons). For such a large animal they had short lives, though. They lived until they were about 30 years old.

*Tyrannosaurus' teeth were up to 15 cm (6 in) long. The back edge of each tooth was sharp and wavy, like a steak knife. This made it easier to slice through meat.*

*Tyrannosaurus' arms may have been small, but its thick bones supported strong muscles.*

## FROM HAND TO MOUTH

With its 1.5 metre (5 ft) skull and teeth the size and shape of a banana, Tyrannosaurus rex could only have been a meat-eater. It had the strongest bite of any animal and could easily crunch through the biggest bones.

Its two fingered arms were tiny, but powerful. Each one could lift 1,000 kilos (1 ton). They may have been used to grab hold of its **prey** as its teeth went to work.

*The American alligator's bite is nearly as powerful as a Tyrannosaurus' bite.*

# PART ONE... THE LAST EGG

THE BABY TYRANNOSAURUS CREEPS QUIETLY THROUGH THE FOREST.

SUDDENLY, SHE IS AMBUSHED BY ONE OF HER BROTHERS. THEY ARE PLAY-HUNTING.

THEY HEAR A NOISE CLOSE BY AND STOP THEIR PLAY-HUNTING.

THEY HIDE AND WAIT.

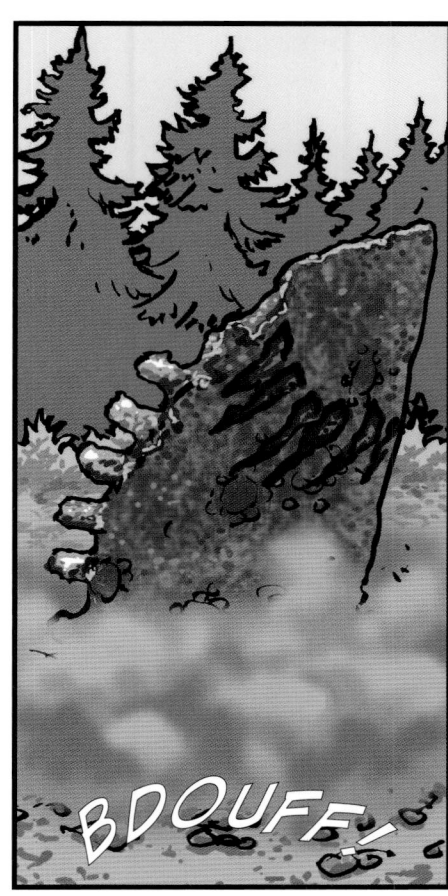

BDOUFF!

THE NOISE WAS MADE BY THE **HATCHLINGS'** MOTHER. SHE HAS BEEN HUNTING FOR REAL AND HAS RETURNED WITH FOOD FOR THEM.

SHARRGH!

HISSSS!

THE MOTHER TYRANNOSAURUS LEAVES THE HATCHLINGS TO THEIR MEAL.

SHE WANTS TO VISIT HER NEST. MOST OF HER EGGS HAVE HATCHED BUT THERE MAY BE SOME LEFT.

SHE PUTS HER NOSE INTO THE NEST AND SNIFFS. IT FEELS TOO WARM. THE EGGS WILL NOT HATCH IF THE NEST BECOMES TOO HOT OR TOO COLD.

SHE BLOWS THE WARM EARTH AWAY FROM THE NEST.

PFHOOOF

THERE IS ONE EGG LEFT.

SHE WILL RETURN TO THE NEST BEFORE IT GETS DARK AND COVER THE EGG IN THE WARM SOIL.

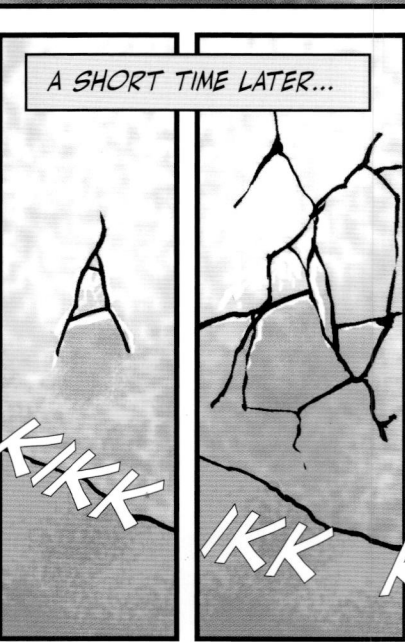

A SHORT TIME LATER...

KIKK IKK

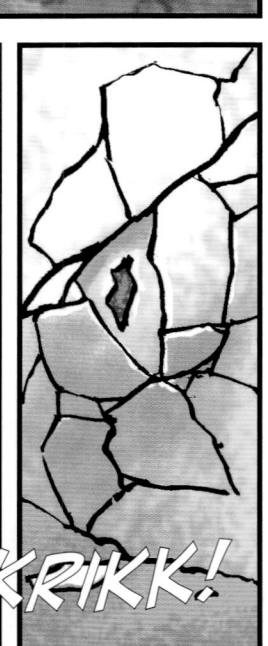

KRIKK!

BREAKING OUT OF HIS EGG HAS MADE THE NEW HATCHLING TIRED.

HIS OLDER BROTHERS AND SISTERS GATHER ROUND.

THEY ARE HUNGRY AGAIN.

THEIR MOTHER ARRIVES JUST IN TIME. SHE GENTLY PUSHES THE HATCHLINGS AWAY FROM THEIR NEW BROTHER.

ARRKK!

THE LAST HATCHLING WILL SOON BE BIG ENOUGH TO PLAY-HUNT WITH HIS BROTHERS AND SISTERS.

# PART TWO... THE PACK

IT IS ONE YEAR LATER. THERE ARE ONLY FOUR HATCHLINGS LEFT. THEY ARE A METRE (3 FT) LONG AND CATCH MOST OF THEIR OWN FOOD NOW.

THE LAST HATCHLING HAS CAUGHT A LIZARD. HIS BROTHERS AND SISTERS ARE TRYING TO TAKE IT AWAY FROM HIM.

THE YOUNG TYRANNOSAURS ARE TOO BUSY ARGUING OVER THE LIZARD TO NOTICE THAT THEY ARE NOT ALONE.

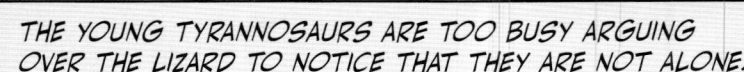

RHARRK!

THE FULLY-GROWN ATROCIRAPTOR IS NO MATCH FOR EVEN ONE OF THE HATCHLINGS. THE YOUNG TYRANNOSAURS TRY TO SCARE IT AWAY.

THEN...

THE ATROCIRAPTOR HAD CALLED TO THE REST OF ITS PACK.

A WHOLE PACK OF ATROCIRAPTORS IS DANGEROUS. THEY WANT THE LIZARD. TOGETHER THEY COULD KILL A TYRANNOSAURUS HATCHLING.

SUDDENLY, FROM THE FOREST...

THUD!

IT IS A CHIROSTENOTES, AND IT IS BEING FOLLOWED.

THUD!

THUD!

ROOARR!

THE ATROCIRAPTORS ARE SCARED AWAY. EVEN THE YOUNG TYRANNOSAURS RUN AS THEIR ANGRY MOTHER CHASES THE CHIROSTENOTES WHO HAS TRIED TO STEAL AN EGG.

THUD!

IT IS THE LAST TIME THE HATCHLINGS' MOTHER WILL COME TO THEIR RESCUE. SHE HAS A NEW NEST AND NEW EGGS TO CARE FOR. THE YOUNG TYRANNOSAURS WILL HAVE TO LOOK AFTER THEMSELVES NOW.

IT IS SEVEN YEARS LATER. THE YOUNG TYRANNOSAURS ARE NOW FIVE METRES (15 FT) LONG. THEY HUNT IN A PACK.

ONCE THEY HAVE SPOTTED THEIR PREY THEY SPLIT INTO TWO GROUPS.

THEY HAVE SEEN A HERD OF PACHYCEPHALOSAURS. ONE PAIR OF TYRANNOSAURS RUNS AT THE PREY.

THE OTHER PAIR WAIT. WHEN THE PACHYCEPHALOSAURS ARE NEAR ENOUGH THEY WILL RUSH OUT FROM THEIR HIDING PLACE AND AMBUSH THEM.

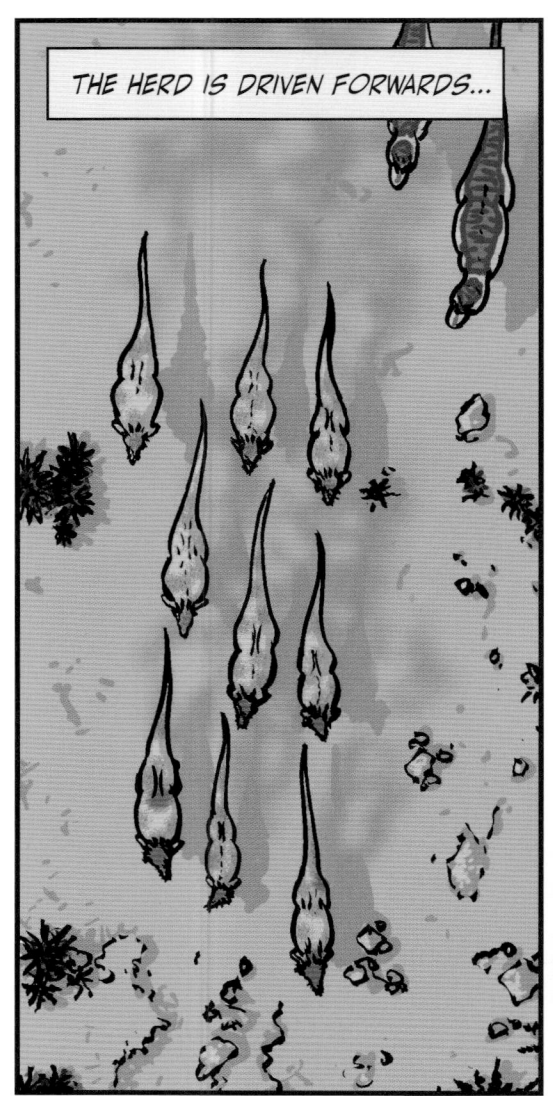

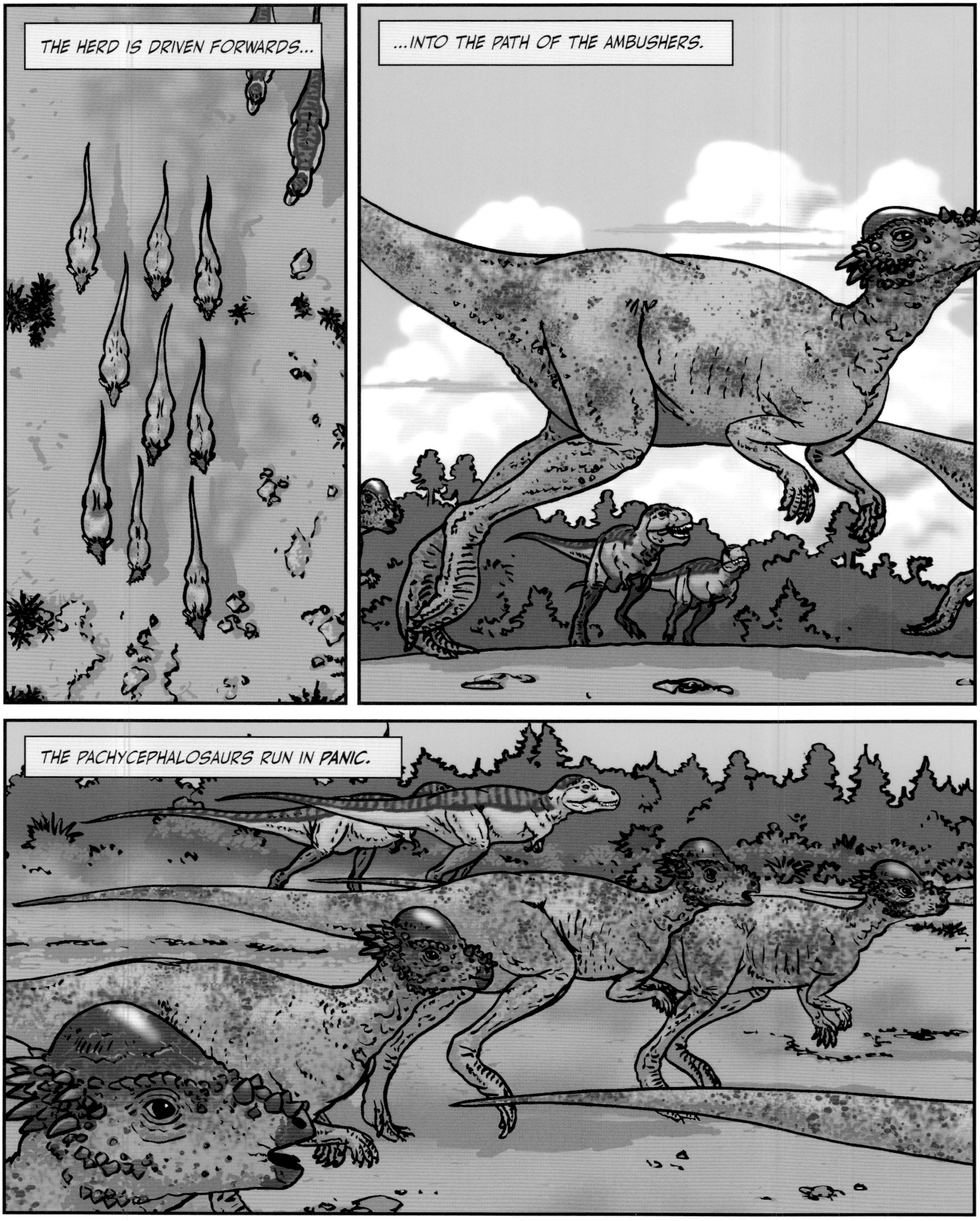

THE HERD IS DRIVEN FORWARDS...

...INTO THE PATH OF THE AMBUSHERS.

THE PACHYCEPHALOSAURS RUN IN *PANIC.*

ONE OF THE PACK CATCHES A STRAY PACHYCEPHALOSAUR, WHEN SUDDENLY...

...THE TYRANNOSAURUS IS HIT BY A CHARGING PACHYCEPHALOSAURUS, AND THEN ANOTHER ONE.

GNARRSH!

DOUFF!!

AGAIN AND AGAIN THEY ATTACK, RUNNING AWAY BEFORE THE TYRANNOSAURUS CAN STRIKE BACK.

THE TYRANNOSAURUS IS BADLY HURT. HE CANNOT STAND UP.

THE OTHERS LEAVE AND FOLLOW THE TRAIL OF THE WOUNDED PACHYCEPHALOSAUR. THEY WILL NEVER SEE THEIR BROTHER AGAIN.

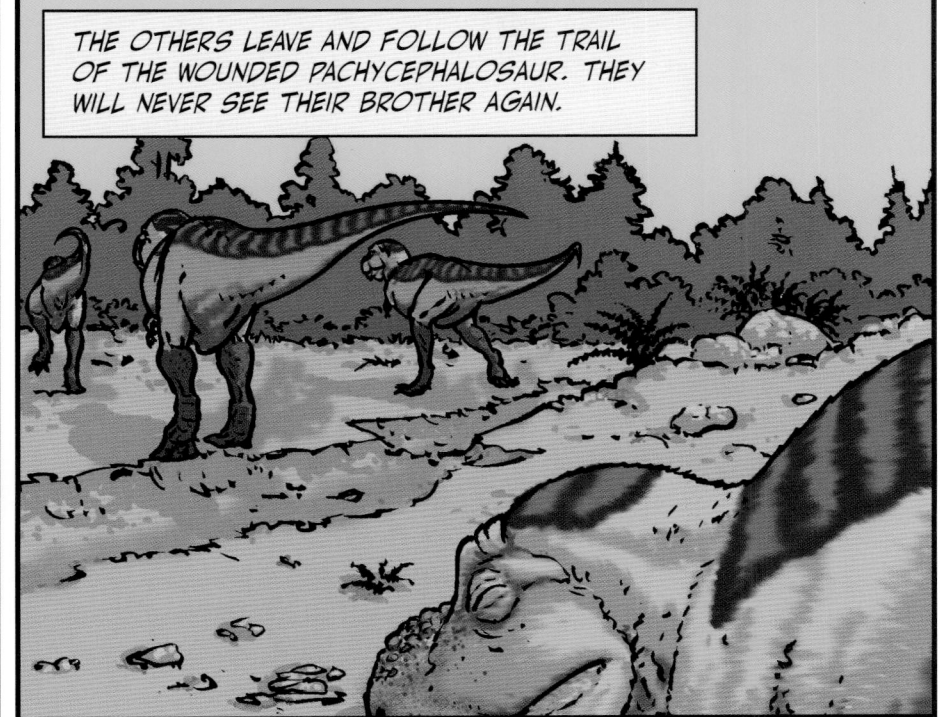

THE TYRANNOSAURS ARE NOW 14 YEARS OLD. THEY ARE GROWING VERY QUICKLY AND ARE ALWAYS HUNGRY. THEY NEED TO HUNT LARGER PREY. THE ALAMOSAURUS IS TOO BIG EVEN FOR AN ADULT TYRANNOSAUR BUT IT IS THE *JUVENILE* THEY ARE AFTER.

TWO OF THE PACK TRY TO KEEP THE ADULT ALAMOSAURUS BUSY.

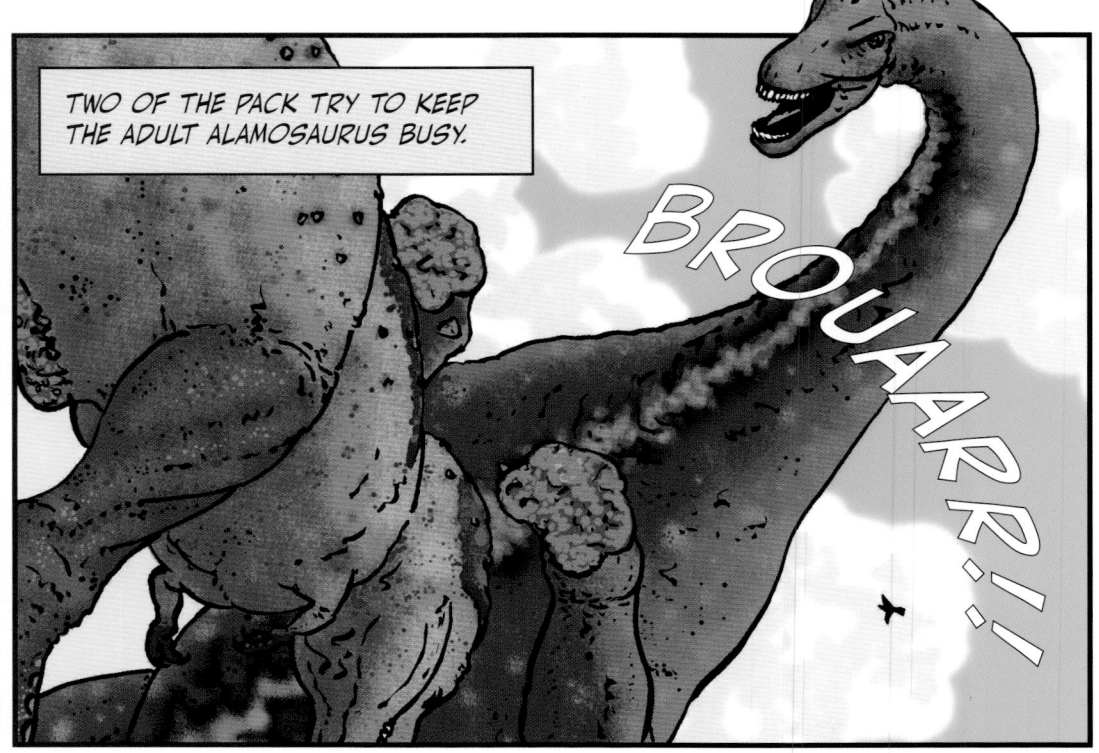

BROUAARR!!

THEY NEED TO BE CAREFUL THOUGH.

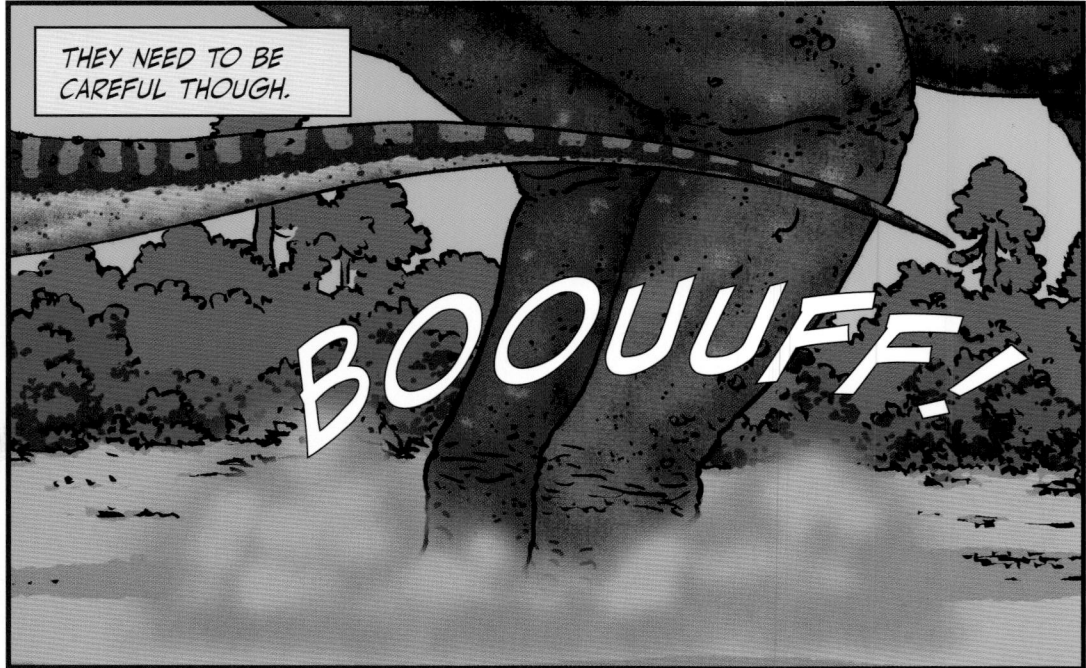

BOOUUFF!

THEY HAVE MANAGED TO SEPARATE THE PARENT FROM THE YOUNG ALAMOSAURUS.

THE YOUNG ALAMOSAURUS IS HELPLESS. THE PACK LEADER MOVES IN.

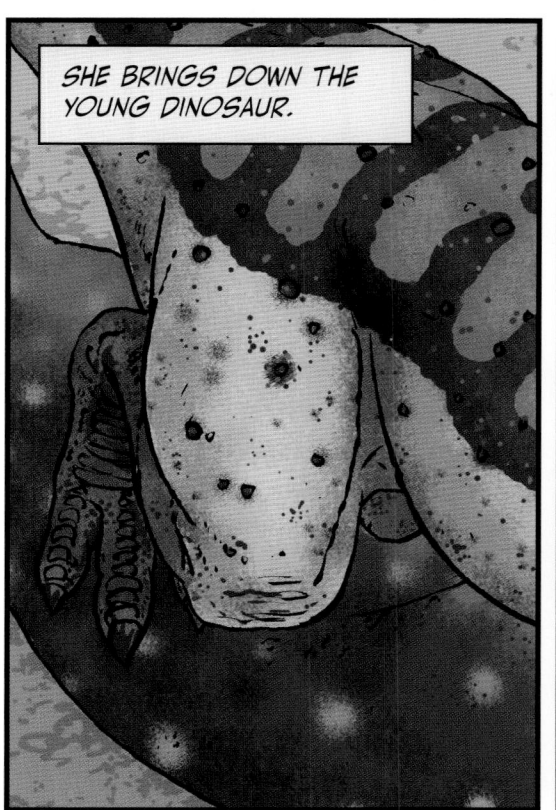

SHE BRINGS DOWN THE YOUNG DINOSAUR.

THE ALAMOSAURUS PARENT REALISES IT HAS LOST AND LEAVES. THE TWO TYRANNOSAURS GO TO GET THEIR SHARE OF THE MEAT.

THE PACK LEADER WILL NOT LET THE OTHERS NEAR THE KILL. SHE WANTS IT ALL FOR HERSELF.

SHE FIGHTS FOR IT.

THE LARGE FEMALE IS TOO BIG FOR THE OTHERS TO BEAT.

THE PACK SPLITS UP.

# PART THREE... HOME TERRITORY

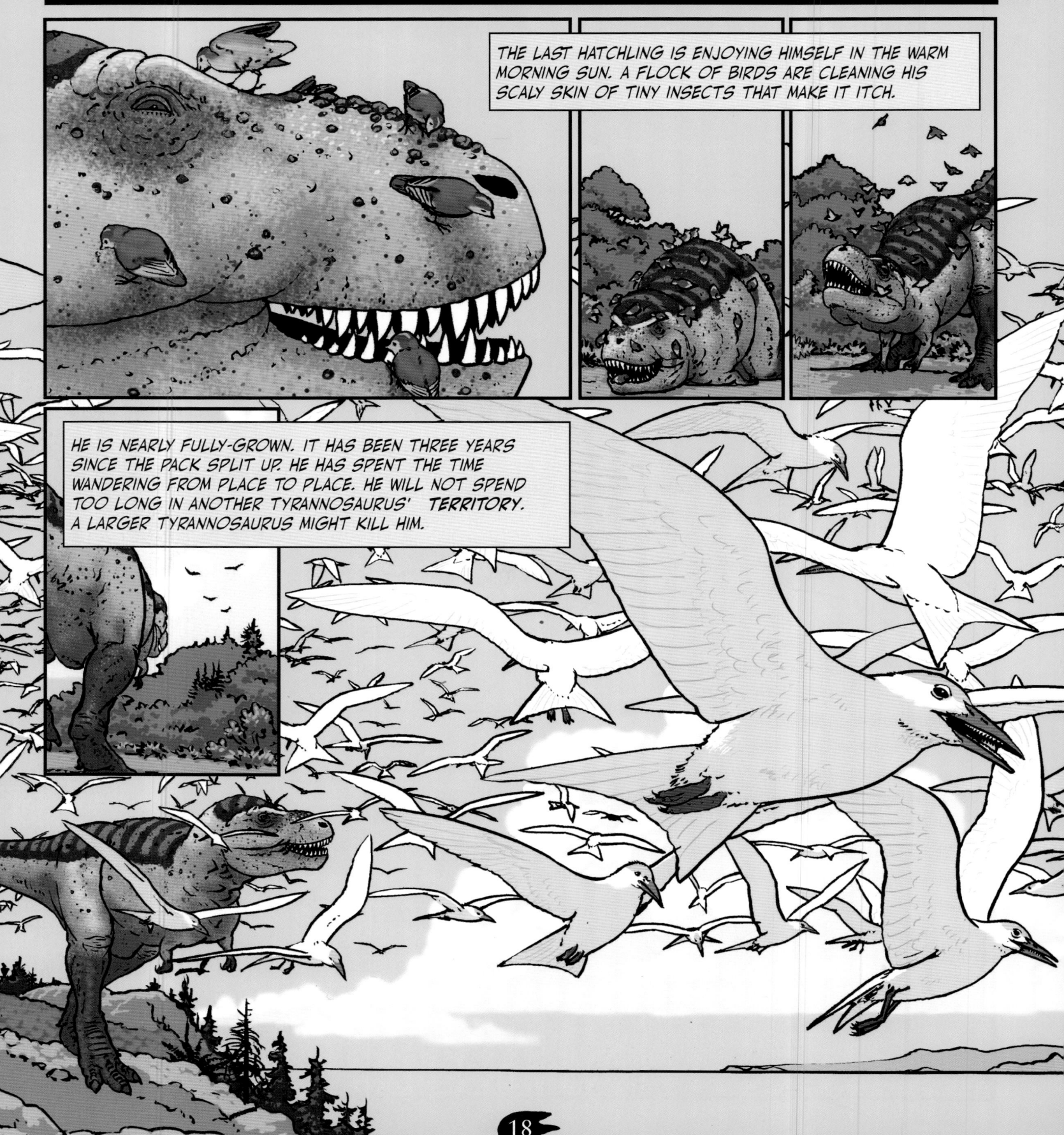

THE LAST HATCHLING IS ENJOYING HIMSELF IN THE WARM MORNING SUN. A FLOCK OF BIRDS ARE CLEANING HIS SCALY SKIN OF TINY INSECTS THAT MAKE IT ITCH.

HE IS NEARLY FULLY-GROWN. IT HAS BEEN THREE YEARS SINCE THE PACK SPLIT UP. HE HAS SPENT THE TIME WANDERING FROM PLACE TO PLACE. HE WILL NOT SPEND TOO LONG IN ANOTHER TYRANNOSAURUS' TERRITORY. A LARGER TYRANNOSAURUS MIGHT KILL HIM.

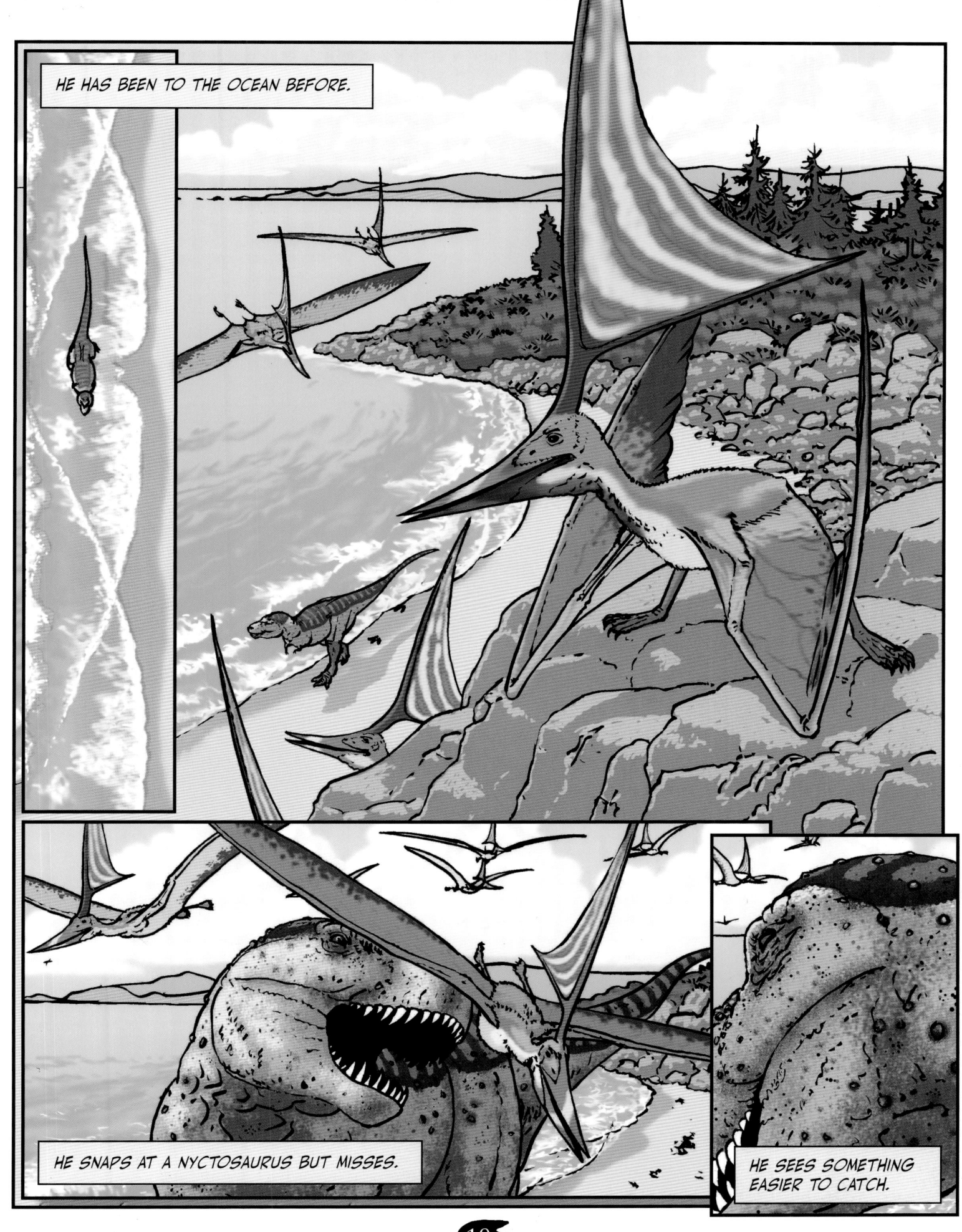

HE HAS BEEN TO THE OCEAN BEFORE.

HE SNAPS AT A NYCTOSAURUS BUT MISSES.

HE SEES SOMETHING EASIER TO CATCH.

A GROUP OF PARKSOSAURUS HAVE LEFT THEIR FOREST HOME.

THE TYRANNOSAURUS MOVES CAREFULLY TOWARDS THE SMALL DINOSAURS. HE CANNOT LET THEM SEE HIM.

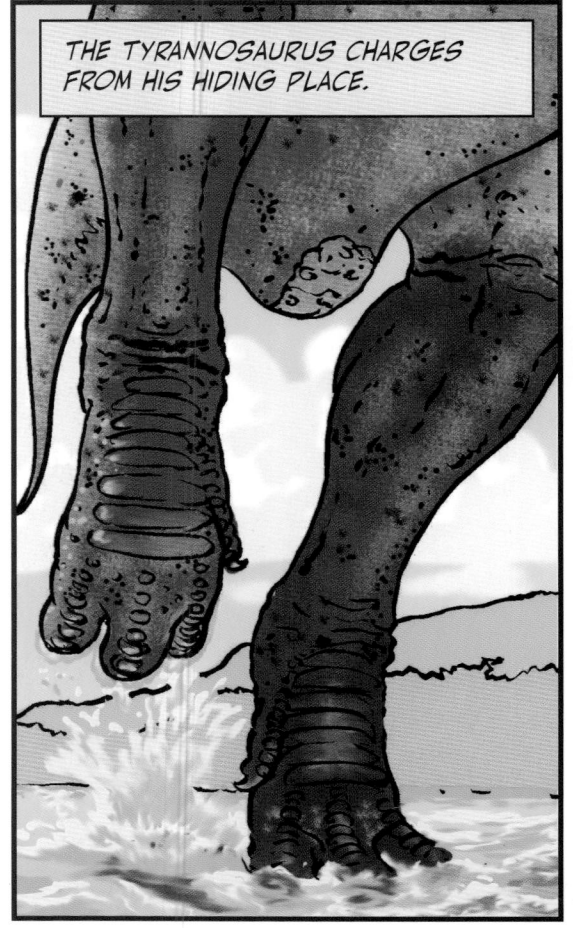

THE TYRANNOSAURUS CHARGES FROM HIS HIDING PLACE.

THE PARKSOSAURUS ARE TOO QUICK. THEY DISAPPEAR BACK INTO THE FOREST.

NOT LONG AGO HE MIGHT HAVE CAUGHT ONE. NOW HE HAS GROWN TOO BIG TO RUN QUICKLY. HE SEES A FLOCK OF ICHTHYORNIS. SOMETHING HAS EXCITED THEM.

THE SEA HAS WASHED UP A DEAD TURTLE.

THE TYRANNOSAURUS DRAGS THE GIANT TURTLE FROM THE WATER.

GER CRUNCH!

THE SHELL OF THE TURTLE IS HARD. THE TYRANNOSAURUS' SIZE HAS MADE HIM SLOW BUT IT HAS GIVEN HIM A STRONG BITE.

HE MOVES INLAND UP A RIVER MOUTH. HE CAN SMELL FRESH BLOOD.

THE SMELL LEADS HIM TO A WOOD. A YOUNG FEMALE TYRANNOSAURUS HAS A DEAD HADROSAUR.

THE FEMALE LETS OUT A WARNING ROAR WHEN SHE SEES THE NEWCOMER.

GROAARR!

THE TWO MEAT-EATERS ARE AS BIG AS EACH OTHER.

GNARRHH!

THE LAST HATCHLING ATTACKS...

ROAARR!

...BUT THE FEMALE IS STRONG AND FIGHTS HARD TO KEEP HER FOOD.

THE LAST HATCHLING BREAKS FREE AND BITES.

ROAARR!

THE WOUNDED FEMALE WALKS AWAY.

THE LAST HATCHLING HAS WON HIS FIRST FIGHT. IT IS TIME FOR HIM TO CLAIM HIS OWN TERRITORY.

# PART FOUR

# THE FIRE

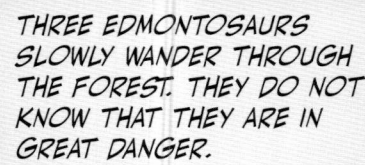

THREE EDMONTOSAURS SLOWLY WANDER THROUGH THE FOREST. THEY DO NOT KNOW THAT THEY ARE IN GREAT DANGER.

THE LAST HATCHLING IS NOW A 20-YEAR-OLD ADULT. HE HAS BEEN WATCHING THE THREE DINOSAURS. HE MIGHT NOT BE ABLE TO RUN QUICKLY BUT HE KNOWS HOW TO AMBUSH THEM.

THE TYRANNOSAURUS WAITS FOR THE RIGHT MOMENT AND CHARGES AT THE EDMONTOSAURS.

GRAHH!

THE EDMONTOSAURUS MANAGES TO WRIGGLE FREE AND RUNS.

WARHHK!

THE TYRANNOSAURUS CHASES AFTER IT.

THE EDMONTOSAURUS DASHES INTO A RIVER.

THE TYRANNOSAURUS DOES NOT FOLLOW. THE AIR SMELLS STRANGE.

THE TYRANNOSAURUS CAN SMELL SMOKE. NOT FAR AWAY A SMALL FIRE HAS GROWN INTO A LARGE ONE. THE FIRE IS MOVING QUICKLY TOWARDS HIM.

ANIMALS THAT USUALLY RUN AWAY FROM HIM RUSH PAST TRYING TO ESCAPE FROM THE FLAMES.

THE TYRANNOSAURUS REALISES HE IS IN DANGER.

THE FIRE IS SPREADING FASTER THAN HE CAN RUN.

ROAROAROAR!

THE TYRANNOSAURUS RUNS THROUGH THE FLAMES...

...AND INTO THE RIVER.

THE FIRE GETS CLOSER AND CLOSER.

THERE IS NOWHERE ELSE LEFT TO GO.

LATER, THE TYRANNOSAURUS COMES OUT FROM BEHIND THE WATERFALL. IT HAS SAVED HIS LIFE.

HE CAN LEAVE NOW THE FIRE HAS DIED DOWN.

ALL THE TREES ARE BURNT. HIS TERRITORY IS COVERED WITH GREY ASH. IT WILL BE MANY WEEKS BEFORE NEW PLANTS GROW AND ANIMALS RETURN.

HE CAN SMELL MEAT.

A HADROSAUR HAS BEEN KILLED BY THE FIRE. IT WILL FEED THE TYRANNOSAURUS FOR SEVERAL DAYS. THEN HE WILL HAVE TO MOVE ON AND FIND A NEW TERRITORY TO RULE OVER.

# FOSSIL EVIDENCE

SCIENTISTS LEARN WHAT DINOSAURS MAY HAVE LOOKED LIKE BY STUDYING THEIR FOSSIL REMAINS. FOSSILS ARE FORMED WHEN THE HARD PARTS OF AN ANIMAL OR PLANT BECOME BURIED AND TURN TO ROCK OVER MILLIONS OF YEARS.

Scientists are not sure whether Tyrannosaurus rex was a hunter or a **scavenger** or both. When an Edmontosaurus skeleton in the Denver Museum, USA, was looked at carefully scientists noticed it had part of its tail bitten away. They saw that the shape of the bite was the same as a Tyrannosaurus' mouth. They also saw that the bones had begun to heal. The Edmontosaurus must have been alive when the Tyrannosaurus attacked it. It must also have escaped the attack. Tyrannosaurus rex may have scavenged but could probably hunt as well.

We do know Tyrannosaurus fought its own kind. Their fossil skeletons show injuries that could only have been caused by another Tyrannosaurus. One skeleton, nicknamed Stan, has a 2.5-centimetre (1-inch) hole in the back of his skull. A Tyrannosaurus tooth fits neatly into it. The bite did not kill him though.

# DINOSAUR GALLERY

ALL THESE ANIMALS APPEAR IN THE STORY.

### Atrociraptor
'Cruel thief'
Length: 1 m (3 ft)
A small feathered dinosaur with a **retractable** claw on each of its first toes.

### Chirostenotes
'Narrow hand'
Length: 2 m (7 ft)
A fast-moving meat-eater with very long hands.

### Nyctosaurus
'Bat lizard'
Wingspan: 3 m (10 ft)
Not a dinosaur but a flying reptile.

### Parksosaurus
'Parks' lizard'
Length: 2.5 m (8 ft)
A small plant-eater with a beak instead of front teeth.

### Pachycephalosaurus
'Thick headed lizard'
Length: 5.5 m (18 ft)
A plant-eater with a very thick and bony skull.

### Alamosaurus
'Alamo lizard'
Length: 21 m (68 ft)
A giant plant-eating dinosaur weighing 27,200 kg (30 tons).

### Edmontosaurus
'Edmonton lizard'
Length: 13 m (43 ft)
A large plant-eater named after the place in Canada where its fossils were first found.

# GLOSSARY

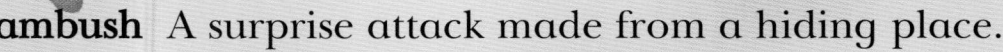

**ambush** A surprise attack made from a hiding place.

**Cretaceous period** The period of time between 146 million and 65 million years ago.

**fossils** The remains of living things that have turned to rock.

**hatchlings** Young animals that have hatched from eggs.

**juvenile** A young animal that is not fully grown.

**panic** To be suddenly scared.

**prey** An animal that is hunted and killed for food by another animal.

**retractable** Something that can be drawn back.

**scavenger** An animal that feeds on other animals that are already dead.

**territory** An area of land that an animal controls.

# INDEX

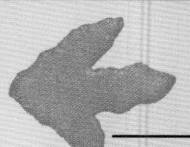 

# Picture History
## of the
## 20th Century

# THE 1970s

## Tim Healey

FRANKLIN WATTS
LONDON • SYDNEY

This edition © 2004 Franklin Watts

Franklin Watts
96 Leonard Street
London
EC2A 4XD

Franklin Watts Australia
45-51 Huntley Street
Alexandria
NSW 2015

ISBN 0 7496 5671 9

First published in 1988

Design: Edward Kinsey
Editor: Sue Unstead
Picture Research: Linda Proud, Jan Croot

Photographs:
Australian Information Office
BBC Hulton
British Airways
British Rail
Camera Press
Chrysalis Records
Design Council
Chris Fairclough
Friends of the Earth
Hutchison Picture Library
Kobal Collection
NASA
Novosti Press Agency
Photoresearchers
Photosource
Popperfoto
Rapho
Science Photo Library
Frank Spooner Library
Sygma
Topham Library
UPI/Bettmann Newsphotos
USDA
WHO
Zefa

# Contents

# Introduction

Coming after the hectic excitement of the so-called Swinging Sixties, the 1970s seemed to many people a time of caution and retreat. One major factor was the world oil crisis which began in 1973. Oil-producing nations suddenly raised the price of oil, causing businesses to fail and trade to slump throughout the world. Large-scale unemployment – unknown for many years – returned to the wealthy nations of the West.

There were other sombre themes. People started to lose confidence in science as they realized the possible hazards of nuclear fuels and pollution. People lost some faith in government, too – especially in the United States, where the Watergate scandal exposed dishonesty at the highest level.

The general mood of disillusionment was caught by the punks who emerged around 1976. Like the hippies of earlier years, they rejected the values of middle-class life. But instead of love and peace they expressed anger and disappointment: a sense that society had cheated them.

There were also some positive things about the 1970s, however. In world politics, for example, the threat of nuclear war receded as the governments of the United States and the Soviet Union pursued a policy of *détente* (the easing of tension). The nightmare of the Vietnam War ended. And China, long suspicious of all outside influence, started opening its doors to foreigners.

In countries of the West, the women's movement gained widespread support. And although the oil crisis may have created shortages, it also taught people to cherish the Earth's natural resources instead of squandering them. Many people continued to prefer "natural" foods – grown without the use of pesticides or artificial fertilizers. Overall, there was a much greater concern for the environment.

In the end it was probably right for people to be more critical – to question modern technology: to sort the good from the bad in new developments. The 1970s may not have been as lively as the previous decade – but perhaps they were more thoughtful.

# Britain in the 1970s

On 1 January 1973, Britain became a member of the Common Market. This is an organization of European nations created to foster co-operation in trade and to bind its members more closely as a community. It was a historic event, because British governments had been trying for many years to gain entry. And there was much discussion too: opponents of membership feared that Britain was giving up too much independence, or that its prosperity would be harmed. Nevertheless, when in 1975 the British people were asked to vote on whether to stay in they replied with a definite "yes".

1973 was important for Britain in other respects too. In that year a strike of coal miners resulted in a state of emergency which was to contribute to the downfall of the Conservative government led by Edward Heath. And from December the first effects of the oil crisis were felt. It was to bring unemployment and high inflation (which causes money to lose its value). With troubles in Northern Ireland and racial tensions in the large cities, Britain had its share of problems.

Nevertheless, there were achievements too. The first oil flowed from Britain's North Sea rigs, and the first high-speed trains ran on Britain's railways. British doctors developed major innovations in the body scanner and test-tube babies (see page 22). And in 1977, when Queen Elizabeth II's Silver Jubilee was held, people celebrated with extraordinary gaiety.

△Newspaper headlines announce that Britain has joined the Common Market on Monday 1 January 1973. Conservative Prime Minister Edward Heath had signed the EEC treaty in Brussels the previous year (EEC stands for European Economic Community – another name for the Common Market).

▷In 1971, to prepare for Common Market entry, Britain changed its old money to decimal currency. Under the old system there were 12 pennies in a shilling, and 20 shillings in a pound. The new system was simpler, having 100 new pennies to the pound. A special organization was set up to aid the changeover.

△In 1977, children celebrate the Queen's Silver Jubilee at a street party in London's East End. It marked the 25th anniversary of Queen Elizabeth II's coronation.

▷The rise of the racist National Front party in the 1970s led to counter-marches by members of the Anti-Nazi League (photographed here in London in 1978).

▽High-speed trains, introduced in 1976, were capable of reaching 143 mph (230 km/h).

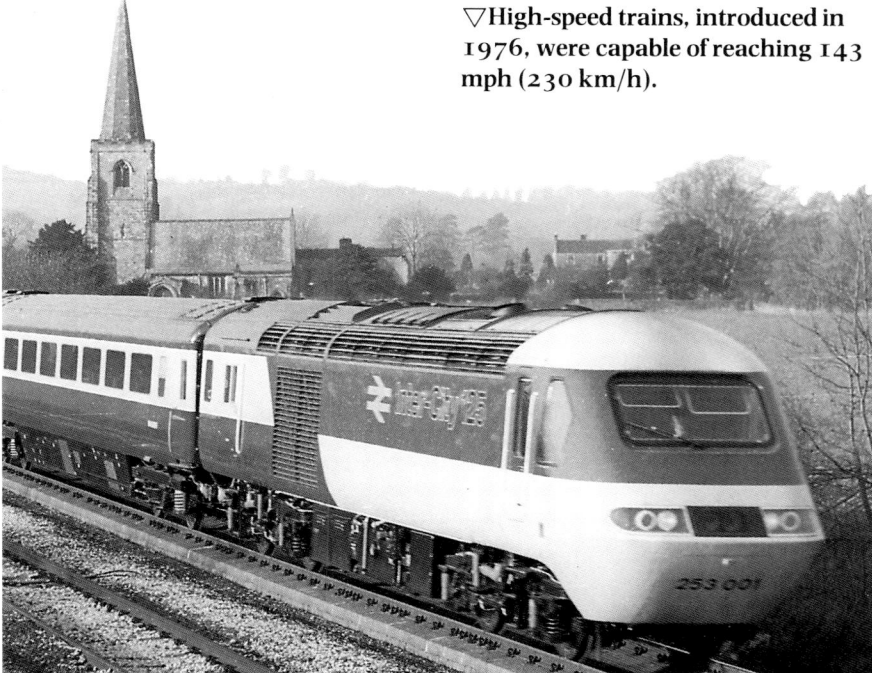

# Prospects for peace

*Détente* is a word often used to describe the world politics of the 1970s. It refers to an easing of tension between nations especially between the Soviet Union and the United States. The process extended to China in February 1972, when President Nixon flew to China for a historic eight-day visit. There he met Chairman Mao, and the trip ended with a joint statement that their two countries would work to achieve normal relations with one another.

Then, in May of the same year, Nixon became the first American president to visit Moscow, where he held talks with Soviet leaders. These resulted in an important pact limiting nuclear missiles: the Strategic Arms Limitation Treaty.

With the American withdrawal from Vietnam in 1973, there were real prospects for world peace. The threat of a catastrophic nuclear war now seemed more remote.

△ With a historic handshake, Richard Nixon meets Chairman Mao during the president's famous visit to China on 21 February 1972. What the president called his "journey for peace" ended more than 20 years of hostility.

△ An ICBM on its launch pad in the United States. ICBM stands for Intercontinental Ballistic Missile, a missile capable of being fired from one continent to another. Carrying nuclear warheads, such weapons present a real threat to world peace. The SALT 1 treaty (1972) put a five-year ban on their testing.

▷ Shovelling grain in Texas. The United States produced bumper wheat crops in the 1970s, and as part of *détente* the government agreed to sell huge quantities to the Soviet Union.

◁In 1976 Vietnam was reunited under a Communist government. Thousands of refugees, known as "boat people", later fled the country in small craft.

▽An American prisoner of war, released by North Vietnam, is reunited with his wife and children in California in 1973.

# The oil crisis

In 1973 Israel and Egypt fought a fierce war in the Middle East. It ended in an uneasy truce, but in time the two old enemies reached a lasting peace agreement, with help from the United States.

In the course of the war, however, oil supplies were disrupted and Arab producers realized that oil was vital to wealthy Western nations as a fuel for transport and industry. It was also the basis of countless chemical products, from paints and fertilizers to plastic bags and even shampoos.

In December 1973 the Organization of Petroleum Exporting Countries (OPEC) vastly increased prices; at the same time they agreed to limit output. Shortages and soaring costs had a disastrous effect on industries throughout the world, and as businesses failed people lost their jobs. Inflation was rife: because everything cost so much more to make and transport, prices of goods soared year after year.

▽Israeli soldiers taken prisoner in the "Yom Kippur" War 1973. The Israelis were surprised by a sudden attack made on a Jewish religious festival.

▷Israeli troops brandish their flag as they mount a counter-attack. By the time of the ceasefire, the so-called Yom Kippur War had reached stalemate.

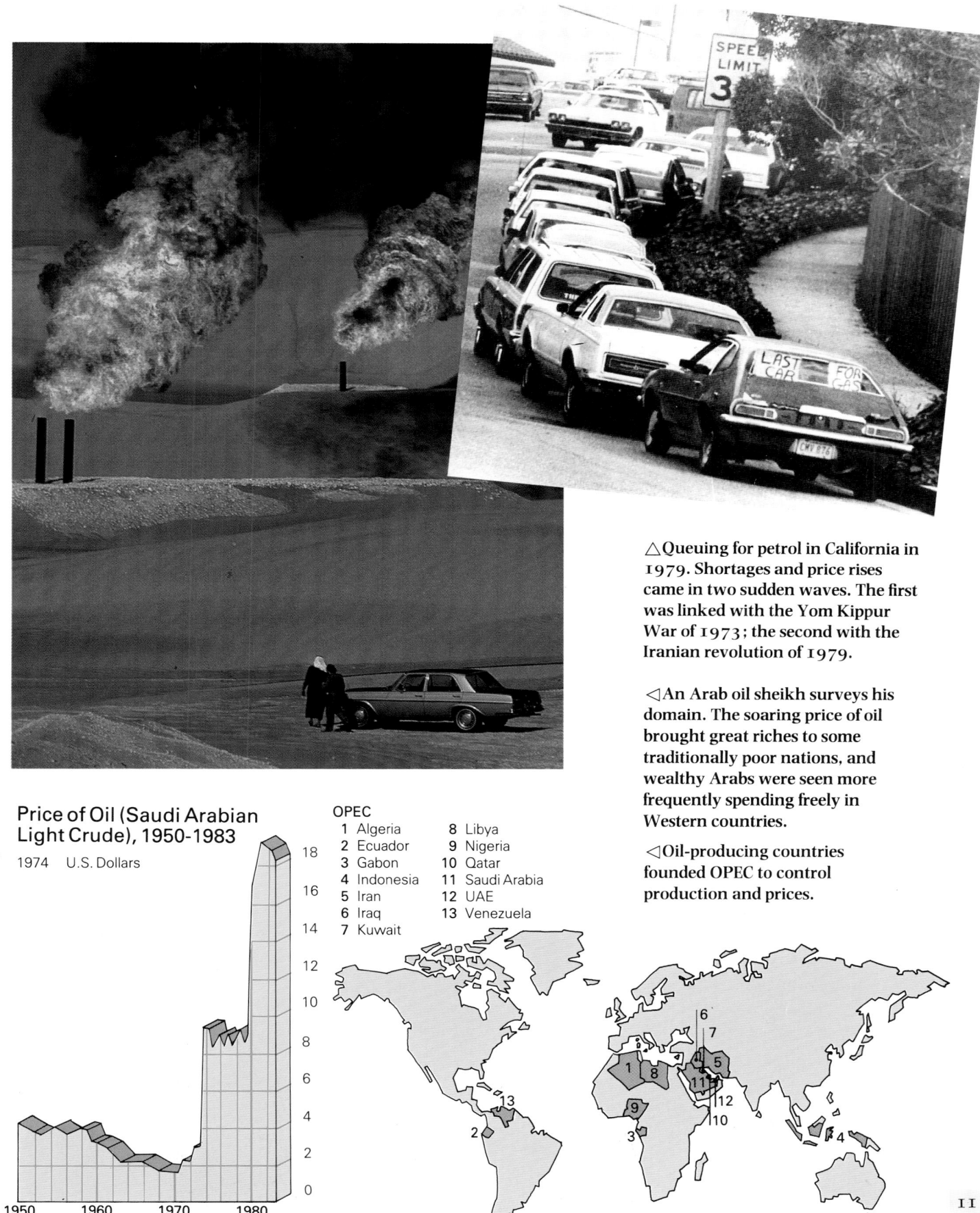

△Queuing for petrol in California in 1979. Shortages and price rises came in two sudden waves. The first was linked with the Yom Kippur War of 1973; the second with the Iranian revolution of 1979.

◁An Arab oil sheikh surveys his domain. The soaring price of oil brought great riches to some traditionally poor nations, and wealthy Arabs were seen more frequently spending freely in Western countries.

◁Oil-producing countries founded OPEC to control production and prices.

## Price of Oil (Saudi Arabian Light Crude), 1950-1983

1974   U.S. Dollars

OPEC
1 Algeria    8 Libya
2 Ecuador    9 Nigeria
3 Gabon    10 Qatar
4 Indonesia    11 Saudi Arabia
5 Iran    12 UAE
6 Iraq    13 Venezuela
7 Kuwait

# The United States on trial

At about 1 a.m. on 17 June 1972, five men broke into the Democratic Party headquarters at the Watergate Complex in Washington, D.C. They were caught and found to be connected with an organization called CREEP (Committee for the Re-Elect the President). Their aim had been to instal eavesdropping devices to spy on President Nixon's opponent in the presidential election of that year.

How much were top Republicans involved? At first President Nixon flatly denied that anyone close to him was implicated. But as journalists investigated the affair, they found even more evidence of "dirty tricks" and of attempts to hush up the Watergate burglary. Some of Nixon's closest advisers were implicated. And although the president persistently denied any personal connection with the burglary or its cover-up, there were calls for him to be impeached (charged with misconduct while holding office).

Meanwhile, Vice-President Spiro Agnew was forced to resign through a separate income tax scandal; it almost seemed as if the United States itself was on trial. In the end, some tape recordings made at the White House confirmed Nixon's knowledge of the Watergate cover-up. Guilty White House staff members were imprisoned, and the president resigned under threat of impeachment.

▷President Nixon goes under the microscope. He had been re-elected president in 1972 in a landslide victory over his Democratic opponent Senator George McGovern, with 520 electoral votes to 17. Then came the Watergate revelations.

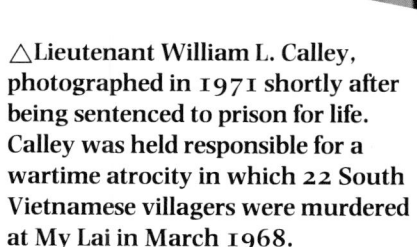

△Lieutenant William L. Calley, photographed in 1971 shortly after being sentenced to prison for life. Calley was held responsible for a wartime atrocity in which 22 South Vietnamese villagers were murdered at My Lai in March 1968.

Watergate shocked and divided American society. The demonstrators at Mercer University in Macon, Georgia (above) call for Nixon's impeachment. But Nixon was forced to resign the presidency and in August 1974 he gave a farewell address in the White House (right) to his Cabinet, aides and staff.

# The terrorists

Bomb blasts, hijackings, kidnappings and assassinations . . . such events were constantly reported in the newspapers of the 1970s. The main wave of terrorism had its origins in the Middle East, where Palestinian refugees from Israeli-held territory lived in crowded camps. Many felt frustrated that the Arab states had been unable to defeat Israel in war. In anger and despair they turned to tactics of terror.

Events began at Rome in July 1968 with the first Palestinian hijack of an Israeli aircraft. And the violence increased over the years as groups elsewhere made contact with Palestinians, sometimes receiving training from them.

The IRA (Irish Republican Army) was active in Britain, the Red Army in Japan, the Baader-Meinhof gang in West Germany and the Red Brigades in Italy. Each group shared a common strategy of creating an outrage to draw attention to their cause.

Probably the most notorious event was the killing of Israeli athletes in Munich, which nearly closed down the 1972 Olympic Games. In response to this and the many other outrages, seven nations, including the United States and Britain, met in Bonn in July 1978 and agreed to tough measures against countries that sheltered terrorist groups.

In September 1970 Palestinian terrorists hijacked three aircraft and flew them to Dawson's Field in Jordan. The 300 passengers taken hostage were eventually released, but the planes were blown up. The event won publicity for the Palestinians, but also led to Arab disunity. King Hussein of Jordan expelled Palestinian groups from his country.

◁A hooded Palestinian terrorist pictured on the balcony of the building in the Olympic village where Israeli athletes were being held hostage in 1972. The Munich incident ended with a gunfight and massacre at a West German airport: 5 terrorists, 11 Israelis and one policeman died by the time the episode was over.

▷Patty Hearst, photographed by security cameras, taking part in a San Francisco bank robbery in 1974. In a curious incident Patricia Hearst, daughter of a multi-millionaire, was kidnapped by an American group called the Symbionese Liberation Army. She was persuaded by them to take part in a bank raid. Captured by the FBI, she was charged and convicted of bank robbery in 1976.

▽An IRA bomb blast at Westminster, the seat of British government. Terrorism claimed hundreds of lives in Northern Ireland, where the IRA's aim was to end British rule.

# The Muslim revival

One of the least expected developments in world affairs of the 1970s was a dramatic return to strict religious fundamentalism among people of the Muslim countries. These are nations that share the Islamic faith, and stretch from North Africa through the Middle East to Pakistan and Bangladesh. Many of them had been under colonial rule in the early years of this century. But with independence and the new riches brought by oil wealth, they regained confidence in their own traditions.

Instead of copying Western styles and values, they returned to the teachings of the Koran, the sacred scripture of Islam. Women were encouraged to wear traditional dress; strict Islamic punishments were revived.

Libya's leader, Colonel Qaddafi, combined strict Islamic practices with revolutionary socialism. Pakistan's General Zia, who rose to power in a military coup of 1977, also revived Islamic puritanism. But the most spectacular changes probably took place in Iran, where in 1979 the pro-Western Shah was overthrown in a fundamentalist revolution which swept Ayatollah Khomeini to power.

The revival disturbed the superpowers of both West and East. And fear of a Muslim uprising in Afghanistan was one reason why in 1979 the Soviet Union sent troops to occupy the country, placing the policy of *détente* in jeopardy.

△The Shah of Iran (Mohammad Reza Pahlavi), depicted on a banknote. As ruler of his country from 1941 the Shah developed strong links with the United States. In 1979, however, violent disorders forced him into exile and an Islamic Republic was set up in Iran.

▷Iranian women, their hair covered in traditional style, display portraits of the Ayatollah Khomeini. In 1979 he returned from exile to lead the Islamic Revolution. His supporters condemned the Shah's regime for corruption and the torture of political opponents.

◁ Muslims in Tehran in prayer. At the time of the American embassy siege, some 2 million people went on to the city streets to express support for the Ayatollah and hatred of the United States.

▽Burning the American flag at the American embassy in Teheran. In November 1979 student supporters of Ayatollah Khomeini occupied the embassy building, taking 63 Americans as hostages. The students were demanding the return of the Shah to face trial for his alleged crimes.

# Transport

The oil crisis revolutionized road transport. Petrol became so costly that it no longer made sense for families to buy huge, large-engined cars. Manufacturers concentrated instead on efficient designs that conserved fuel.

Thoughts about the economy also affected the Anglo-French Concorde. This supersonic airliner entered service in 1976, cutting travel time between London and New York to just over three hours. But costs were high and the plane carried comparatively few passengers. A rival American proposal for supersonic transport was scrapped because of the expense, and no new Concordes were built in the 1980s. More successful was the Boeing 747 or Jumbo Jet, which entered service in 1970. It carried up to 490 passengers in its wide body, providing cheap air travel for many ordinary people who had never flown before.

In 1971 the *Queen Mary* (bottom), one of the great transatlantic liners of the past, took on a new role. She opened as a floating museum, hotel and conference centre at Long Beach, California.

Inside a Japanese car factory (below). Manufacturers in Japan specialized in cheap, small-engined cars, which suited the fuel-conscious 1970s. Japan's exports were so successful that they threatened the car industries of other nations.

▷Flight and cabin crew celebrate as the first American Boeing 747 Jumbo Jet goes into service in 1970. The roomy cabin was capable of carrying twice as many passengers as the earlier Boeing 707 jet airliner.

▽A Concorde aircraft photographed in 1975. The supersonic plane was beautifully designed with a long, pointed nose that drooped on take-off and landing to allow the pilot to see ahead. However, costs were huge and some countries objected to the aircraft because of the noise it made as it broke the sound barrier.

# Science and technology

The first microprocessor was patented in the United States in 1971. It was an entire computer processor contained on a single silicon chip, and the device permitted a whole new generation of computers to be built. Computers were smaller, cheaper and more efficient than any earlier examples, and towards the end of the 1970s everyday life was transformed with the mass production of microchips.

Lasers also came into wide use. A laser is a device that produces a beam of intensely pure light. It can cut through metal, perform eye surgery, or create the extraordinary three-dimensional images known as holograms. In 1977 the first moving film using holography was demonstrated in the Soviet Union.

▷ A laser at work in industry. The beam is here being used to drill holes in jet engine turbine blades.

▽ Holograms are photographs that require laser lighting to record them, and to use them to produce 3-D images. The boy here can walk around the woman's head and see it from different angles as he moves. The first holograms were pale, ghost-like images in a single colour.

▷ This picture illustrates advances in computer circuits. The large brown board comes from a computer of 1963, and has bulky transistors. The smaller blue board comes from the late 1960s and includes integrated circuits (the black rectangular components). Later, further miniaturization was achieved; the integrated circuits in the top left-hand corner come from an IBM machine of the 1970s.

◁ A scientist clones plants. Cloning attracted great attention in the 1970s. It is a means of making exact duplicates of living things from a single cell, or by taking cuttings. In the 1970s it was announced that scientists had managed to clone frogs. Would humans be next? In 1978 a journalist caused a sensation by claiming that he had helped a millionaire to produce clone offspring; the claim was a hoax, however.

▷ Scientists experimented in the field of plant genetics, hoping to create new varieties of crops which would help to feed the world's hungry people. One result was the "sunbean" shown here – a cross between a bean and a sunflower. Another was the "pomato", a cross between a potato and a tomato (which unfortunately proved to be poisonous).

# Health and medicine

During the 1970s much publicity was given to the harmful side-effects of certain modern drugs. Thalidomide, in particular, a sedative used in Europe in the 1960s, was found to produce deformed babies. A legal battle was fought in Britain during the 1970s by parents seeking compensation from the drug's manufacturers.

But despite more critical attitudes to modern medicine, some major breakthroughs were made. In 1979 Britain's Geoffrey Hounsfield and American Allan M. Cormack were awarded a Nobel Prize for devising the EMI scanner, a device that produces a complete image of the inside of the body. The term "bionics" was coined for some exciting innovations in matching electronic equipment to bodily functions. And in 1978 two British doctors, Robert Edwards and Patrick Steptoe, achieved the first test-tube birth. A baby girl, Louise Brown, was born following laboratory fertilization of her mother's egg.

Equally impressive in a different way was the work of the World Health Organization (WHO). Over many years it carried out a worldwide programme of vaccination against smallpox – and succeeded. In 1980 the world was officially declared free from smallpox; for the first time medical science had eliminated a major disease.

◁Newspapers announce the first test-tube birth. The mother had long been childless because of a defect in her Fallopian tubes; now, science had helped give her a baby.

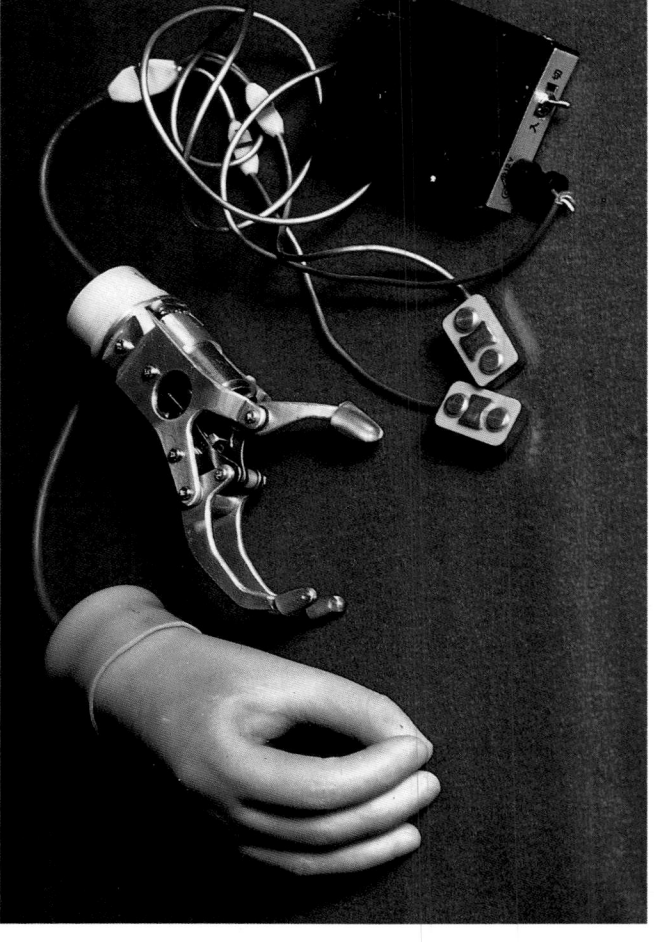

▽An artificial hand created by electronics. Developments like this inspired TV's popular *The Six Million Dollar Man*, a programme about a man with "bionic" limbs.

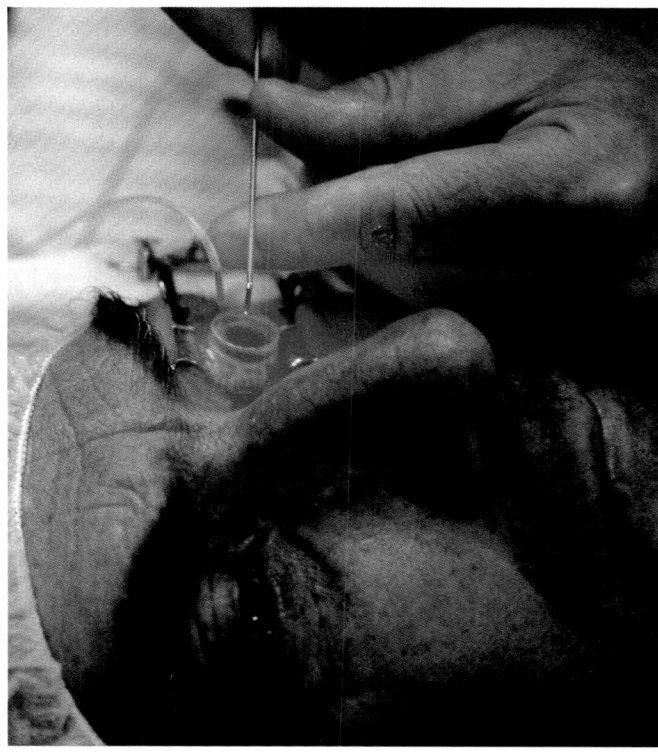

△A laser used in eye surgery. In this operation a laser beam is directed on to the eye through a fibre-optic tube. (Fibre optics is a branch of science in which light is passed along flexible glass threads less than a millimetre thick.)

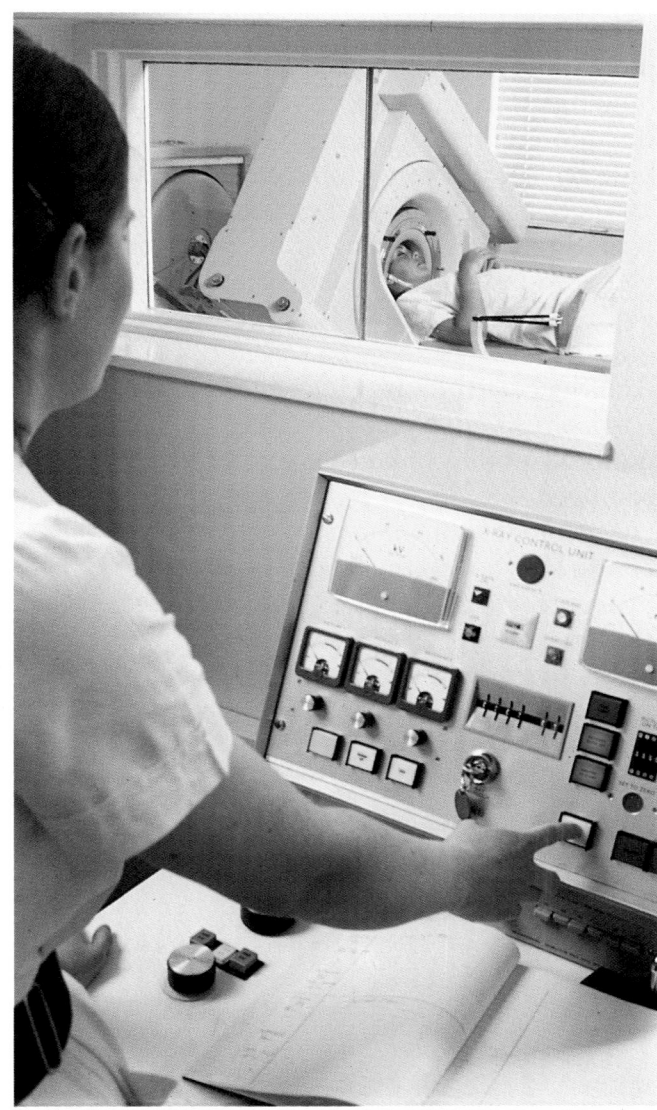

▷A patient enters a body scanner. This electronic device is capable of scanning the body for defects which then show up in a computer image on a TV screen. Dr Geoffrey Hounsfield and Allan M. Cormack were awarded the 1979 Nobel Prize for this invention.

▷Vaccinating against smallpox in Uganda in 1975. The worldwide campaign to wipe out the disease was launched in 1967 by the World Health Organization (WHO), an agency of the United Nations. It succeeded in the 1970s; on 8 May 1980 smallpox was officially declared eradicated.

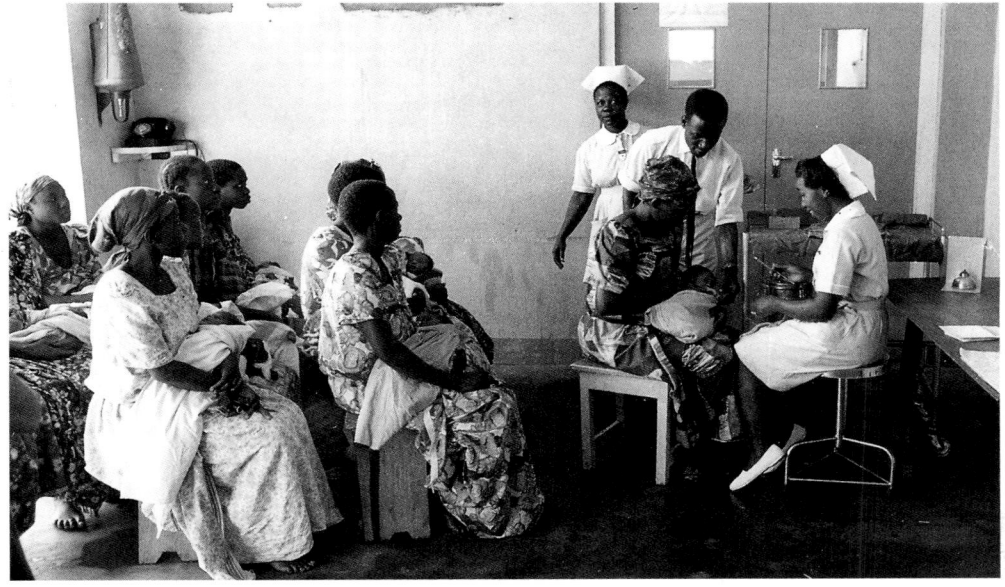

# Space conquest

After the historic Apollo 11 mission took the first men to the Moon in 1969, more manned lunar landings were made. By 1972, twelve astronauts had been on the Moon's surface, exploring not only on foot but using lunar roving vehicles, or Moon buggies as they were known. Altogether some 382 kg (842 lb) of lunar rocks and dust were brought back to Earth. But the cost of the flights was enormous and the public came to question their benefits. In December 1972 American astronauts Eugene Cernan and Harrison Schmitt made the sixth and final manned landing; plans for further ones were scrapped.

Missions to the planets by unmanned craft continued, however, and much effort was concentrated on the development of space stations. These are craft designed for research, partly to test humans' long-term abilities to live and work in space. The first of them was the Soviet Salyut (meaning "salute"), launched in April 1971. The United States replied by launching its own space station, Skylab, in May 1973; it was at first manned by teams of astronauts but afterwards left empty in orbit. Skylab re-entered the Earth's atmosphere in July 1979 and crashed, amid much publicity, strewing debris across the Western Australian desert.

Rivalry between the United States and Soviet Union never wholly disappeared, but hopes of co-operation were raised in July 1975 with the first international space docking. An American Apollo and Soviet Soyuz craft linked up while they were orbiting Earth. Their astronauts conducted joint experiments, shared meals and held a news conference together. It was a heartening celebration of *détente* – but has sadly never been repeated.

◁In July 1971, Apollo 15 astronauts David Scott and James Irwin made the fourth manned Moon landing, taking with them the first American Moon buggy. It can be seen to the right of the picture. The tall "umbrella" device is a long-range antenna; the vehicle was also equipped with a TV camera and a drill for taking rock samples.

▽American stamps issued in 1975 to commemorate the American/Soviet link-up of Apollo and Soyuz spacecraft.

US 10c

APOLLO SOYUZ 1975

APOLLO SOYUZ SPACE TEST PROJECT

10c

UNITED STATES · 1975

◁Astronauts aboard Skylab. The space stations sent up in the 1970s were large craft equipped for long, manned missions. They allowed the crew to live and work in space on a variety of projects. For example, astronauts studied weather patterns on Earth, collected particles from space and planted seeds in their laboratories to see how plants grew in weightless conditions.

Throughout the 1970s the Soviet Union explored Venus with its Venera probes (below). The first landing was in 1970, but in 1975 Veneras 9 and 10 soft-landed and sent back the first pictures of a planet whose surface temperature turned out to be a scorching 470°C (880°F).

Two American Viking spacecraft landed on Mars in 1976 (below left), and tested for signs of life, but no evidence of Martians or any living thing was found.

# The global clean-up

Even before the 1970s, people were expressing concern about the ways in which modern life was damaging the environment (the world around us). Fumes from motor vehicles, for example, were polluting the atmosphere; factory chemicals were spoiling rivers; and thoughtless killing of animals threatened the survival of some species.

By 1970 the environment had become a major issue. And in the following years many laws were passed in the industrial nations concerning the cleanness of water and air, the conservation of nature, and the control of dangerous wastes. A United Nations Conference on the Human Environment was held in Stockholm in 1972, and some agreement was reached on international issues such as the pollution of the seas.

Fierce argument, however, surrounded the future of nuclear energy. And it was dramatized by an accident at the Three Mile Island reactor near Harrisburg, Pennsylvania, in March 1979.

△New Yorkers participate in the first Earth Day on 22 April 1970. The date was chosen for mass demonstrations against pollution and was observed by millions of Americans nationwide.

▷A Swedish girl demonstrates in 1972 against the litter of modern society. Activists campaigned against cans, bottles and other containers that could not be re-used.

BRING BACK RETURNABLES
Friends of the Earth

26

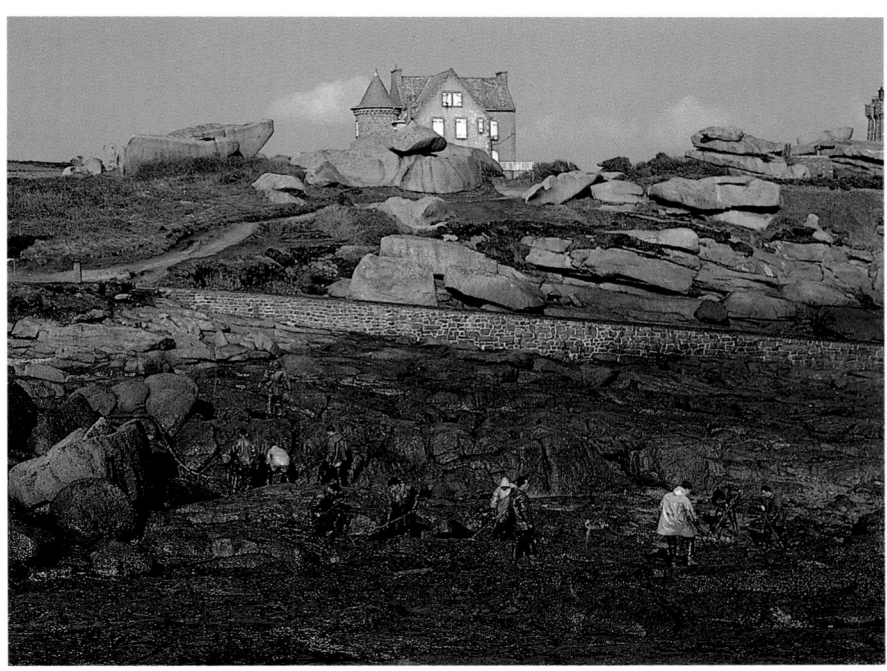

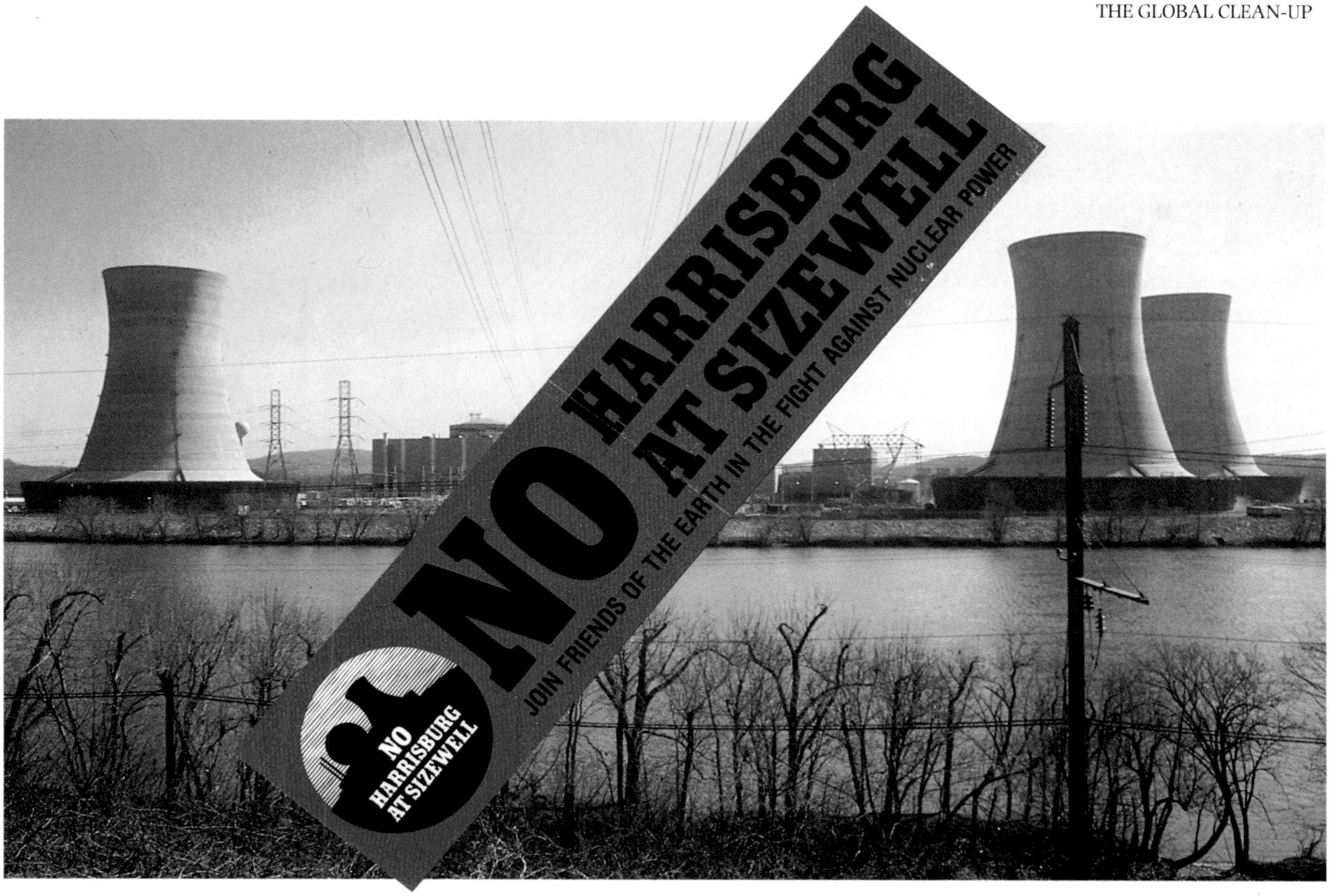
NO HARRISBURG AT SIZEWELL
JOIN FRIENDS OF THE EARTH IN THE FIGHT AGAINST NUCLEAR POWER
NO HARRISBURG AT SIZEWELL

△The nuclear reactor at Three Mile Island, Pennsylvania. In March 1979 a failure in the cooling system caused radioactive gases to escape from the plant. They threatened the population of nearby Harrisburg, a city of 68,000 people, and led to a mass evacuation of the area.

△A sticker issued by opponents of nuclear power questions the safety of the British nuclear power station at Sizewell. The Harrisburg incident caused people throughout the world to question the future of the nuclear industry – its hazards as well as benefits.

The threat to the seas: oil spilled from a wrecked supertanker, *Amoco Cadiz* (below left), polluted French beaches on a horrific scale in 1978.

Whales were threatened with extinction by extensive overfishing. To protect them a sanctuary was set up in the Indian Ocean in 1979.

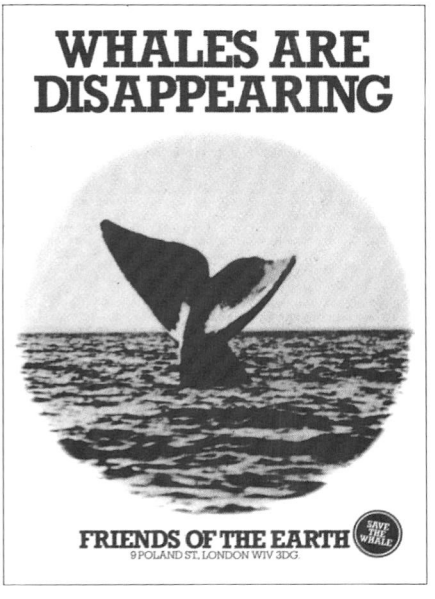

WHALES ARE DISAPPEARING
FRIENDS OF THE EARTH
9 POLAND ST. LONDON WIV 3DG
SAVE THE WHALE

# Exploring alternatives

Was the modern world going terribly wrong? The oil crisis of the 1970s and fears for the environment made some people challenge fundamental ideas about industrial society and look for alternative approaches to living.

Instead of burning the Earth's reserves of coal and oil, for example, people suggested harnessing the clean, natural energies of the Sun, wind and tides. Instead of packaged, processed food people looked for healthier nutrition. And instead of consulting modern doctors with their "scientific" cures, many people tried alternative forms of medicine. The old Chinese art of acupuncture became popular; to cope with stress people attended yoga classes instead of taking tranquillizers. Overall many ideas, once thought "eccentric" won widespread acceptance as the 1970s progressed.

△Experimental solar cars, which converted sunlight into electricity, appeared in the 1970s. This is an Israeli example of 1977.

▽The biggest solar plant of the time was a 5 megawatt furnace at Albuquerque, New Mexico, which was completed in 1977.

Yoga (above) became popular in the 1970s. It originated as an ancient Hindu discipline designed to train followers for spiritual perfection. In Western countries, however, it was often used simply as a means of relaxing the mind and body.

A London health food store (above right) photographed in 1975. Such stores started to open in many countries as people became more concerned about the chemicals in modern foods.

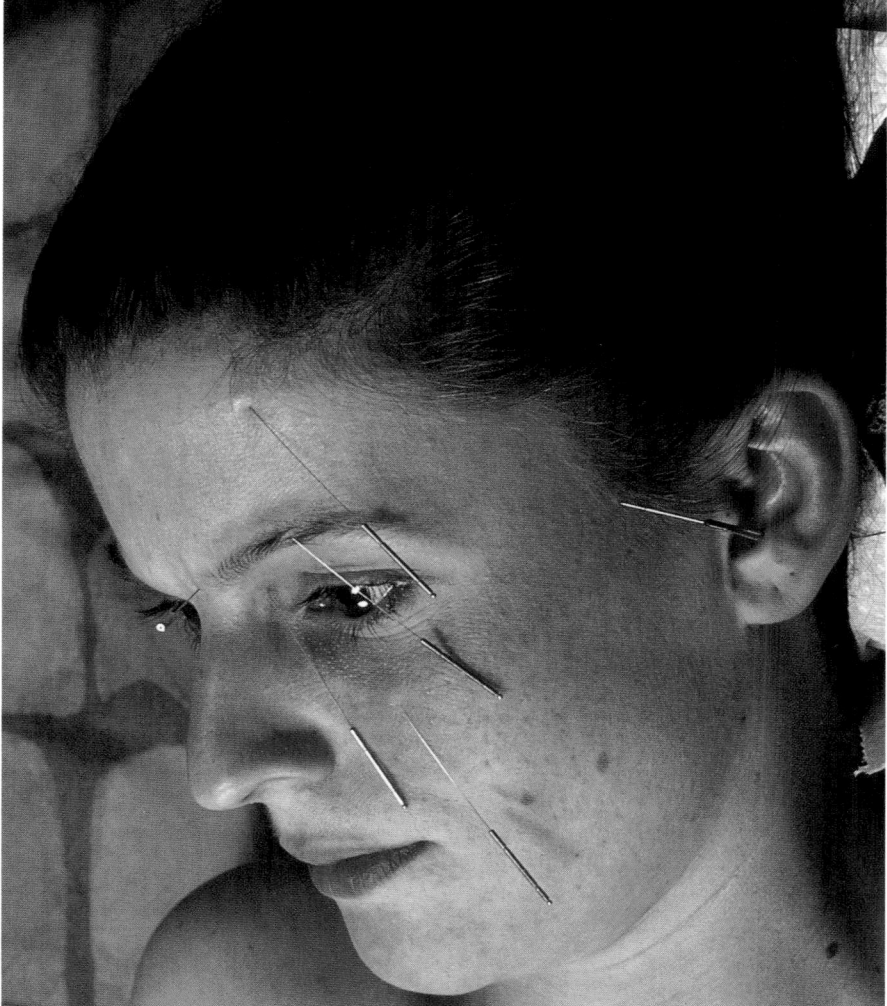

▷ An acupuncturist treats a woman for headaches. According to traditional Chinese beliefs, needles inserted in certain key places can assist a balanced flow of energy in the body. Western scientists have often doubted such claims, but it is possible that the needles do stimulate the brain's production of natural painkillers known as endorphins.

29

# The women's movement

In most democratic countries women had the right to vote long before the 1970s opened. But that did not mean that they shared true equality with men. Girls were generally expected to grow up with one ambition: to become a wife and a mother. Men held almost all the positions of higher authority in society.

A new feminist movement grew up to press for changes both in the law and in attitudes. In 1966, for example, a National Organization for Women (NOW) was founded in the United States, and in 1969 a Women's Liberation Workshop was set up in Britain. By the 1970s they were having a real impact on society.

Stunts made headlines: demonstrators burned their bras or disrupted beauty contests (which feminists believed depicted women as pretty toys for men). But activists also campaigned for equal pay and job opportunities, and for the right to abortion and contraception.

Success in changing the law varied from country to country. In the United States, an Equal Rights Amendment (ERA) banning discrimination on the grounds of sex was passed by the Senate in 1972, but failed to get the necessary votes for ratification. Nevertheless, many new achievements reflected women's changing roles: in 1970 the first American women generals were appointed; in 1975 the first woman scaled Everest (Japan's Junko Tabei); and in 1979 Margaret Thatcher became Britain's first woman prime minister.

▷**Women of the 1970s march for freedom in the United States (right) and Britain (below). Their clothing says almost as much as their banners. Feminists often dressed simply – in jeans and a T-shirt for example. They opposed such fashions as lipstick and high heels that made life awkward and uncomfortable.**

◁A young woman campaigns for the right to abortion, a key issue to feminists. Abortion means ending a pregnancy, and most feminists believe that the mother should have the final right to decide about this.

▽An American stamp celebrates International Women's Year, 1976.

Women are trained in the use of grenades at West Point in 1977 (below left), the year that the famous American military academy first opened its doors to women.

Australian writer Germaine Greer (below) was a leading figure in the new feminist movement.

# New products

A host of new gadgets became available to consumers during the 1970s, including pocket calculators and digital watches (which show numbers instead of hands on a dial). The first video recorders also appeared, and home entertainment was transformed with the arrival of video games and pre-recorded video cassettes. The first video film rentals were offered by Sears, Roebuck in the spring of 1972; by the end of the decade millions of tapes were being rented annually for home viewing.

Miniaturization of electronic equipment was another major theme. By 1979, television sets with screens as small as 5 cm (2 in) across were being manufactured.

△The Sinclair Microvision was the world's smallest television set in the 1970s. The first flat-screened pocket TVs were also patented (1979), but they did not go on sale until the 1980s.

◁The first digital watches went on sale in 1971; these are later examples, dating from 1977 and 1978. Digital watches use small quartz crystals to operate electronic circuits (unlike the mechanical wind-up watches previously used).

▷An early pocket calculator made by the Italian firm of Olivetti. The first electronic pocket calculators were made in 1970 and, like this example, printed out their results on specially treated paper. However, they were quickly transformed by the development of liquid crystal displays (LCDs), which show numbers on display panels. LCDs were adapted for both pocket calculators and digital watches.

◁ Whilst most goods were getting smaller, some were growing in size. The ghetto blaster was carried on shoulders and was capable of emitting a very high volume of music.

▷ The Sony Walkman of 1978 was the first personal stereo cassette player.

33

# Fashion and clothes

The fashionable look in the early 1970s can be thought of as a hangover from the decade which went before. Young men still wore their hair long; some young women wore hot pants, as if trying to continue the 1960 mini-skirt vogue with its high hemlines. Flared trousers and platform shoes were also popular in the 1970s.

Fashion was transformed after 1976, however, by the punk revolution. For shock effect punks cut their hair short and spiky; sometimes in Mohican style or dyed in vivid colours. Chains, zips and safety pins were worn as clothing accessories – the style was very harsh and aggressive. Of course, not everyone copied the extremes.

▽Short hot pants were often worn with long "maxi" coats, as in this outfit designed by Ted Lapidus in 1971.

◁Platform shoes were popular in the early 1970s. They were worn by men as well as women – often with flared bell-bottom trousers (the photograph dates from 1972).

◁Diane Keaton and Woody Allen in a scene from *Annie Hall* (1977), a film which greatly influenced women's fashion. The heroine set a taste for comfortable "mannish" clothing such as tweed jackets, waistcoats and baggy trousers.

▽Zandra Rhodes, photographed here in 1977, was a designer who adapted the styles of youthful punks to the fashion scene. Startling colour contrasts, metallic zips, chains and safety pins were all part of the look.

# Pop and rock music

At the beginning of the decade pop music was a major industry whose stars earned enormous sums of money, performing at giant concerts with expensive light shows and speaker systems. Performers such as T. Rex and David Bowie celebrated the sparkling grandeur of the whole business with what became known as "glitter rock". At their most adventurous, some of the acts brought an exciting space-age feel to popular music, using electronic synthesizers and lasers for stage lighting.

But no group quite filled the gap left by the break-up of the Beatles in 1970, and rock music seemed to have become far removed from the realities of life. People reacted with a taste for instant nostalgia in the revival of simple hits from past decades. Also against the trend for "glitter bands" was reggae, a raw, pulsing music that originated in Jamaica's shanty towns.

But the most dramatic new phenomenon was punk music, which arrived in 1976 with a wave of young bands spearheaded by the Sex Pistols. The punks deliberately set themselves against the long-haired "dinosaurs" of the rock business. Their own music was cheap and harsh, with lyrics often designed to shock.

△David Bowie brought both strangeness and style to pop music in the early 1970s with such songs as *Starman*, *The Jean Genie* and *The Spiders from Mars*.

◁Bob Marley, a Jamaican singer, achieved a worldwide following for reggae with his group the Wailers, after the success of their first single *No Woman No Cry* in 1975. He also won attention for his Rastafarian faith. Originating in Jamaica, it is based on reverence for the former Ethiopian emperor Haile Selassie (whose title was Ras Tafari). Followers wear their hair in long, twisted strands known as dreadlocks.

◁ John Travolta, seen here in the hit film *Saturday Night Fever* (1978), brought a new style of music and dancing to the young rock scene.

▽ The Sex Pistols were the most notorious of the 1970s punk groups. They first entered the charts with their raucous *Anarchy in the UK* in December 1976, and reached the top ten next year with *God Save the Queen*, released during the Silver Jubilee celebrations. Lead singer Johnny Rotten (John Lydon) is in the centre of this picture, flanked by guitarists Glen Matlock and Steve Jones.

△ Blondie, with lead singer Debbie Harry, was among the most successful American groups associated with punk music. They had hit singles in 1979 with *Heart of Glass* and *Sunday Girl* – more polished songs than many earlier punk products.

# Films and television

Satellite communications allowed live television pictures to be flashed from just about anywhere in the world to anywhere else. In 1972, a record 1,000 million people watched transmissions from the Munich Olympics. And television now had such a grip on the world population that the old cinema industry was widely expected to die.

In fact, that did not happen. For one thing, movie-makers were still able to create films with sensational special effects which television studios could not hope to copy. The science fiction blockbuster *Star Wars* (1977), for example, broke all box office records.

Movie-makers also tackled some issues – such as race, sex and violence – more explicitly than television producers were permitted to. And it was found that young people were still keen cinema-goers. Films such as the nostalgic *American Graffiti* (1973) and the disco smash *Saturday Night Fever* (1978) were great hits. Overall, the film industry did surprisingly well: by 1979 in both the United States and Britain *more* cinemas were open than in 1970.

△*Shaft* (1971), starring Richard Roundtree, was important in its day as the first major film to have a black private detective as its hero. It was a great box office success, and led to two movie sequels as well as a television series.

◁The robots C-3PO and R2-D2 were many people's favourite characters in *Star Wars*, directed by George Lucas. In the 1970s the film broke all money-making records. The special effects were created with the most up-to-date film technology, including computer-driven cameras.

△The team of BBC's *Monty Python's Flying Circus* broke many barriers in TV comedy with its zany humour.

▷ Peter Weir's *Picnic at Hanging Rock* (1975) a haunting film set in 1900 started a new wave of Australian movies which won world-wide acclaim.

▽*Jaws* (1975), about a man-eating shark, was both horrifying and hugely successful.

# Sports

It often takes time for a sporting fad to win widespread popularity. Major skateboarding competitions had been staged occasionally since as early as 1966, but it was only in the mid-1970s that the craze became popular throughout the world. Similarly, enthusiasts had long been running to keep fit; but it was only in the 1970s that jogging became widespread. Even President Jimmy Carter participated – although he was to collapse on one run in 1979, amid much publicity.

Sports superstars included Swedish tennis ace Björn Borg and black heavyweight boxer Muhammad Ali, the only man to win the world title three times (1964, 1974 and 1978). The American swimmer Mark Spitz won a world record of seven gold medals in the 1972 Munich Olympic Games.

▽With the skateboarding craze, special courses were built to protect youngsters from accidents in the streets. Records were set: in 1977 a high jump of nearly 1.5 m (5 ft) was achieved by one American skateboarder.

Marathons (below) became hugely popular in New York, London and elsewhere as more and more people took up jogging to keep fit. (A marathon is a race along roads over a standard distance of 42.195 km or 26 miles, 385 yards.)

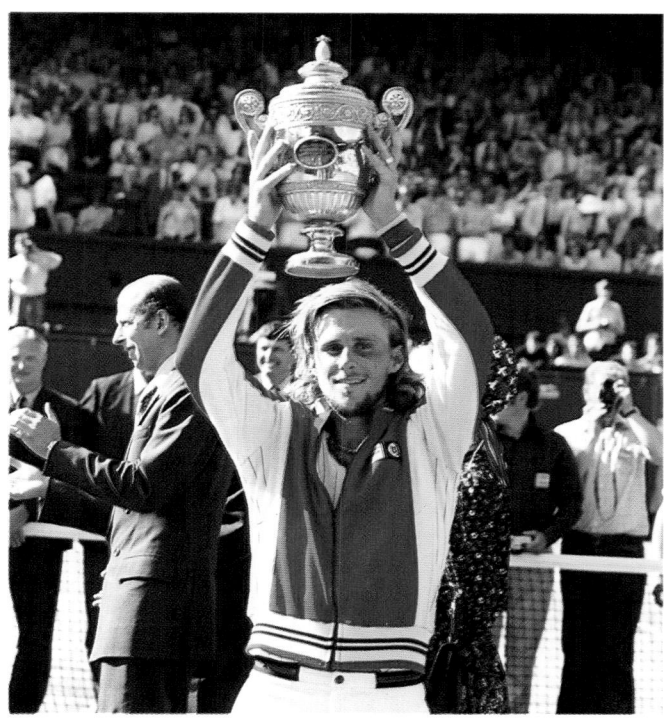

△Björn Borg wins at Wimbledon in 1979. Sweden's tennis ace won the men's singles title at Wimbledon five times between 1976 and 1980 – a record for the 20th century.

Teenage Soviet gymnast Olga Korbut (above right) won many admirers for her performance at the Munich Olympics of 1972. She also took two gold medals – one of them for her work on the balance beam (shown here).

▷Arsenal skipper Frank McLintock holds the FA Cup aloft after his team's 2–1 victory over Liverpool in the Final of 1971. Winning at Wembley gave Arsenal the Cup and League "double" – it was one of only two doubles then achieved in the 20th century (Tottenham Hotspur had performed the same feat in 1961).

# Design and the arts

Some spectacular new buildings were completed in the 1970s, changing the skylines of many of the world's cities. But in other respects, art and design seemed to turn away from abstraction. Traditional styles of painting, for example, received more attention than they had for many years, and experimental forms of writing tended to give way to more orthodox styles treating some of the big issues of the day.

Feminist authors Germaine Greer and Erica Jong dealt with women's themes. Journalists Bob Woodward and Carl Bernstein won fame for their investigations into the Watergate affair. And perhaps the most famous writer of the time was the Soviet author Aleksandr Solzhenitsyn. His works exposed the abuses of the Soviet labour camp system, and led to his expulsion from his home country in 1974.

△ Opened in 1973, Sydney Opera House in Australia is considered to be one of the architectural wonders of the modern world. The shell-roofed building was designed in 1957 by Danish architect Jörn Utzon, and took 16 years to complete at a cost of 14 times the original estimate. The main hall has 2,690 seats.

◁ The World Trade Center, New York City, being built in 1970. Completed the following year, it rose higher than New York's Empire State Building to become the world's tallest building at 411 metres. Its twin towers astonished people for their stark simplicity. On 11 September 2001 tragedy struck when terrorists flew two aeroplanes into the twin towers, with a loss of almost 3,000 lives.

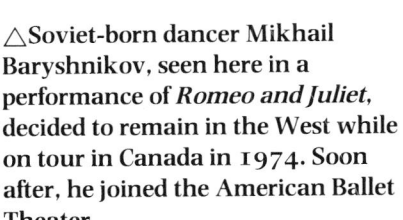Soviet-born dancer Mikhail Baryshnikov, seen here in a performance of *Romeo and Juliet*, decided to remain in the West while on tour in Canada in 1974. Soon after, he joined the American Ballet Theater.

Soviet writer Aleksandr Solzhenitsyn (above right) was awarded the Nobel Prize for Literature in 1970. His major work published after his 1974 expulsion from the Soviet Union was *The Gulag Archipelago*.

▷English artist David Hockney at work in his studio. In the 1970s he won international fame for a style characterized by fine figure drawing.

# Personalities of the 1970s

**Agnew, Spiro** (1918-1996), American Republican politician. As vice-president under Nixon from 1969 to 1973, he was an outspoken opponent of liberals and radicals. He was forced to resign in a tax scandal, which also resulted in a suspended prison sentence.

**Allende, Salvadore** (1908–73), president of Chile from 1970, was the first democratically elected Marxist head of state in the West. His regime was opposed by the United States and by right-wingers at home, and he was killed in a military coup in 1973.

**Amin, Idi** (1925-2003), president of Uganda from 1971 to 1979, expelled the country's large Asian community and was notorious for his brutal regime. Amin was ousted and fled the country in 1979.

**Begin, Menachem** (1913-1992), Israeli prime minister from 1977 to 1983, shared the Nobel Peace Prize (1978) with President Sadat of Egypt for his contribution to a Middle East settlement.

**Bowie, David** (1947– ), born David Jones, British pop singer noted for his stylish, ever-changing image.

**Brezhnev, Leonid** (1906–82), Soviet statesman, emerged from the party leadership team to dominate Soviet government throughout the 1970s.

**Callaghan, James** (1912– ), British Labour prime minister (1976–79) whose government faced high inflation and declared a 5 per cent guideline for wage increases but was defeated following a series of strikes in what was known as the "winter of discontent".

**Carter, Jimmy** (1924– ), American Democratic president from 1977 to 1981, came to power in the wake of the Watergate crisis and promised more open government. He helped to negotiate peace between Egypt and Israel, but lost popularity through failure to cope with inflation, unemployment and the hostage crisis in Iran.

**Deng Xiao-Ping** (1904-1997), vice-premier of China from 1977, was a major influence for reform and increased contact with the West.

**Ford, Gerald** (1913– ), American Republican president from 1974 to 1977, had been vice-president and came to power on Nixon's resignation, facing high inflation due in part to Arab oil price rises.

**Gandhi, Indira** (1917–84), Indian prime minister from 1966 to 1977 and from 1980 to her assassination in 1984. After allegations of corruption and repression, she declared a state of emergency in India in 1975 but was defeated in the 1977 election.

**Greer, Germaine** (1939– ), Australian writer and feminist best known for her book *The Female Eunuch* (1971).

**Heath, Edward** (1916– ), British Conservative prime minister from 1970 to 1974, who took Britain into the Common Market. After fuel shortages caused by the Arab oil crisis, and an overtime ban by miners, he was forced to introduce a three-day working week.

**Hockney, David** (1937– ), British artist influential in reviving interest in good drawing and naturalistic portraits.

**Hua Guo-feng** (1921– ), Chinese prime minister (1976–80) who with Deng Xiao-ping made efforts to modernize China after Mao's death.

**Hussein, Ibn Talal** (1935-1999), King of Jordan 1953-99 and a moderate Arab leader who in 1970-1 expelled Palestinian guerrilla groups from his country.

**John Paul II** (1920–) born Karol Wojtyla, Polish Catholic Churchman who in 1978 became the first non-Italian pope since the 16th century.

**Kissinger, Henry** (1923- ), American foreign policy adviser and secretary of state from 1973 to 1977.

**Indira Gandhi**

**Pope John Paul II**

**Margaret Thatcher**

**Mao Tse-tung** (1893–1976), Chinese Communist leader from 1949 until his death. In the 1970s his revolutionary influence on society waned, and his death was followed by moves to modernize and develop contacts with the West.

**Marley, Bob** (1945–81), Jamaican reggae singer and symbolic figure to many young blacks struggling against oppression in Western society.

**Meir, Golda** (1898–1978), Israeli prime minister from 1969 to 1974, who governed the country at the time of the Yom Kippur War. She resigned soon after its conclusion.

**Mugabe, Robert** (1924–  ), Black Zimbabwean politician and a leader of the Patriotic Front which waged guerilla war against Ian Smith's government in Rhodesia.

**Nixon, Richard** (1913-1994), American Republican president from 1969 to 1974. Although conservative in background, he surprised many by supervising withdrawal from Vietnam and pursuing *détente* with China and the Soviet Union. He was forced to resign because of the Watergate scandal.

**Qaddafi, Muammar al-** (1942–  ), Libyan leader who came to power in a military coup (1969) and used Libya's oil wealth to aid Palestinian guerillas and other revolutionary and terrorist organizations.

**Sadat, Anwar al-** (1918–81), Egyptian president from 1970 until his assassination in 1981 by a fundamentalist Moslem group. He led his country in the Yom Kippur War (1973). He later visited Israel, and his work for a long-term settlement in the Middle East earned him the Nobel Peace Prize jointly with Israel's Prime Minister Begin.

**Sex Pistols,** major British punk rock group. Key members included Johnny Rotten (John Lydon; 1956–  ), and Sid Vicious (John Ritchie; 1958–1979), who died of a drug overdose while awaiting trial in the United States on a murder charge.

**Smith, Ian** (1919–  ), prime minister of Rhodesia (now Zimbabwe), whose rebel government proclaimed the country a republic in 1970. Throughout the next decade his government fought a losing battle with black guerillas of the Patriotic Front.

**Solzhenitsyn, Aleksandr** (1918–  ), Russian author who won worldwide attention for novels critical of the Soviet regime, including *One Day in the Life of Ivan Denisovich* (1962).

**Somoza, Anastasio** (1925–80), Nicaraguan president whose oppressive dictatorship was overthrown by left-wing Sandinista guerillas in 1979.

**Thatcher, Margaret** (1925–  ), British Conservative politician, elected first woman prime minister of Britain in 1979.

**Wilson, Harold** (1916-1995), British Labour prime minister (1964-70; 1974-76). In 1975 he supervised a British referendum on whether to stay in the Common Market. He resigned in April 1976.

**Yamani, Ahmed, Sheikh** (1930–  ), Saudi Arabian minister responsible for petroleum who through OPEC exerted worldwide influence in regulating oil prices.

**Young, Andrew** (1932–  ), American diplomat, the first black American ambassador to the United Nations. Appointed by Jimmy Carter, he was forced to resign in 1979 after a controversial meeting with a representative of the Palestinian Liberation Organization.

**Zia, General Mohammed** (1924–88). President of Pakistan who came to power in an army coup of 1977 which overthrew President Bhutto. Zia postponed elections, introduced strict Islamic law, and presided over Bhutto's execution.

**James Callaghan**

**Edward Heath**

**Harold Wilson**

# The 1970s year by year

## 1970

- American forces enter Cambodia to strike at enemy bases in the Vietnam War; four students are shot dead during anti-war demonstrations at Kent State University, Ohio.
- Palestinian terrorists blow up aircraft on Dawson's Field, Jordan; King Hussein declares war on Palestinian groups in his country.
- Salvadore Allende becomes Marxist president in Chile.
- Aleksandr Solzhenitsyn is awarded the Nobel Prize for Literature.
- Edward Heath is elected prime minister in Britain.
- Americans celebrate the first Earth Day.
- The first Boeing 747 "Jumbo Jets" enter transatlantic service.
- The first pocket electronic calculator is devised.
- The first liquid crystal display is patented.
- Brazil wins soccer's World Cup in Mexico.

## 1971

- American bombers strike at North Vietnamese targets, ending the 1968 bombing halt; in the United States, Lieutenant Calley is convicted of murder for his part in a massacre of Vietnamese civilians.
- East Pakistan breaks away from West Pakistan to become the independent state of Bangladesh; war is fought between India and Pakistan.
- Idi Amin comes to power in a military coup in Uganda.
- Independence year for Qatar and Bahrein.
- First British soldier is killed during the new wave of troubles in Northern Ireland.
- Decimal currency is introduced in Britain.
- Voting age is lowered to 18 in the United States.

- The World Trade Center opens in New York.
- Soviet Union launches the first space station, Salyut 1.
- First microprocessors are produced.
- Digital watch is introduced.
- First body scanner is devised.
- Germaine Greer publishes *The Female Eunuch*.

## 1972

- President Nixon visits China and the Soviet Union. Strategic Arms Limitation Treaty (SALT 1) is signed; American wheat sales to the Soviet Union are announced.
- Munich Olympics are marred by a terrorist massacre.
- United Nations Conference on the Environment is held in Stockholm.
- Five men are arrested for breaking into the Watergate building. Britain signs the Common Market treaty (for entry the following year).
- Thirteen civilians are killed by British troops in Northern Ireland in "Bloody Sunday" disorders; Britain takes over direct rule of the provinces.
- The last Apollo Moon landing is made by American astronauts.
- The first video games are devised.

## 1973

- President Allende is assassinated in Chile.
- Vietnam ceasefire is announced; the last American troops leave the country.
- Vice-president Spiro Agnew resigns in the United States.
- Watergate trial opens; top Nixon aides are implicated.
- Egypt and Syria attack Israel in the Yom Kippur War; fighting ends in deadlock.
- Arab oil producers announce a ban on oil exports; then raise prices, triggering a world economic crisis.

- Coal miners strike in Britain; a state of emergency and a 3-day working week are proclaimed.
- Independence year for the Bahamas.
- United States launches Skylab 1.
- Sydney Opera House opens.
- Sears Tower, Chicago, becomes the world's tallest building, at 443 m (1,454 ft).

## 1974

- President Nixon resigns after impeachment hearings begin in the Watergate case; Gerald Ford becomes president, issuing an unconditional pardon to Nixon.
- Military dictatorship ends in Greece and democratic government is restored.
- Cyprus is partitioned into Turkish and Greek regions.
- Emperor Haile Selassie is deposed in Ethiopia.
- Aleksandr Solzhenitsyn is expelled from the Soviet Union.
- Labour government of Harold Wilson is elected in Britain.
- American spacecraft Mariner 10 transmits the first close-up pictures of Mercury.
- West Germany wins soccer's World Cup in West Germany.

## 1975

- All of Vietnam comes under Communist control.
- Communist Khmer Rouge take over in Cambodia.
- Helsinki Pact is signed by 35 nations, promising to respect human rights and national frontiers.
- Spain's dictator, General Franco, dies; monarchy returns under Juan Carlos.
- Christians and Muslims fight a civil war in Lebanon.
- Independence year for Angola, Mozambique and Papua New Guinea.

- Patty Hearst is captured by FBI agents in the United States.
- Britain votes by referendum to stay in the Common Market.
- Oil starts to flow from Britain's North Sea rigs.
- Apollo-Soyuz link-up by American and Soviet spacecraft celebrates the spirit of *détente*.
- Soviet Venera craft soft-land on Venus, sending back the first pictures from its surface.

# 1976

- Jimmy Carter is elected US president.
- United States celebrates its Bicentennial.
- Chairman Mao dies in China; the new leadership of Hua Guo-feng and Deng Xiao-ping hastens steps to modernize and develop contacts with the West.
- Israeli commandos free hijack hostages in a raid on Entebbe airport.
- Independence year for the Seychelles.
- Harold Wilson resigns in Britain and is succeeded as prime minister by James Callaghan.
- American Viking spacecraft soft-lands on Mars.
- Concorde enters service.
- Britain introduces high-speed trains.
- Sex Pistols enter the British record charts; punk music wins national attention.
- Soviet Union dominates the Montreal Olympics.

# 1977

- Egypt's President Sadat visits Israel to meet Prime Minister Begin in a historic attempt to establish peace in the Middle East.
- General Zia comes to power in an army coup in Pakistan.
- United States launches two Voyager spacecraft.

- President Jimmy Carter pardons Vietnam draft evaders.
- Murderer Gary Gilmore is executed in the United States, marking the use of capital punishment for the first time since 1967.
- Britain celebrates Queen Elizabeth II's Silver Jubilee.
- World's largest solar furnace opens at Albuquerque in New Mexico.
- *Star Wars* is released, becoming the most successful film of the decade.

# 1978

- President Carter presides over the Camp David conference between Prime Minister Begin and President Sadat, resulting in the *Framework for Peace* agreement.
- American Senate votes to hand Panama Canal over to Panama by the end of the century.
- Mass suicide of a religious cult is reported from Jonestown, Guyana.
- Aldo Moro, former Italian Prime Minister, is murdered by terrorist Red Brigades in Italy; a Bonn meeting is held by seven nations seeking agreement to combat international terror.
- John Paul II becomes the first Polish pope.
- Wreck of the tanker *Amoco Cadiz* results in massive oil spillage along the French coast.
- First test-tube baby is born in Britain.
- Muhammad Ali wins the world heavyweight boxing title for a record third time.

# 1979

- Iran is shaken by civil unrest: the Shah flees; Ayatollah Khomeini returns from exile; hostages are seized as students occupy the American embassy in Teheran.
- SALT 2 arms treaty is signed but withdrawn after Soviet troops invade Afghanistan.

- Vietnamese troops occupy Cambodia, overthrowing the repressive regime of the Khmer Rouge; war is fought between China and Vietnam.
- Idi Amin flees Uganda following an invasion by Tanzanian troops and Ugandan exiles.
- Rhodesian peace talks lead to promise of an independent Zimbabwe under majority rule.
- Margaret Thatcher becomes prime minister in Britain.
- Major accident occurs at the US nuclear plant at Three Mile Island near Harrisburg, Pennsylvania.
- American space station Skylab falls to Earth in Western Australia.

# Index